TO WHO… JOURNAL ARISING?

A 1 YEAR DAY PLANNER

for revealing the source within you that's better than any object, drug, relationship or experience

KELLY CREE & JESSICA MULLEN

Published 2022 by Kelly Cree and Jessica Mullen.

ISBN
9781387497386

First Edition November 2022

What is School of Life Design?
School of Life Design (SoLD) is a curriculum for recognizing present moment awareness, training attention and undoing social conditioning. Combining the principles of design with elements of magick, meditation, and manifestation, SoLD makes interactive guides for harnessing the creative power of thought and emotion.

Founded in 2010 by Kelly Cree and Jessica Mullen, SoLD utilizes the principles of design as a framework for shaping life experience. **Gratitude** is the use of *emphasis*: focus on what you like and what you want more of. **Mental codes** (or mantras) create peaceful mental *rhythm*. **Consciousness** is the *balance* of doing, thinking, feeling and being. **Intention** is the purposeful *movement* of energy. **Visualization** generates new *patterns* of thought and expectation. **Transmutation** creates joy out of the *contrast* of pain. **Channeling** reveals the *unity* and connectedness of all things.

When used deliberately, these tools enable you to create and experience the reality you prefer. In each moment, you are faced with a design decision: where do you focus your awareness? With daily practice of SoLD's ever-evolving methodology for lucid living, you will experience the manifestations, synchronicities and miracles you desire. Design your reality instead of the other way around; only you are the creator of you.

Learn more at
www.schooloflifedesign.com

"We have searched for so long in objects, substances, activities, states of mind and relationships for peace and fulfilment. Although the acquisition or experience of any of these brings our search temporarily to an end and, as a result, gives us a brief taste of the peace and fulfilment for which we long, they do not last.

It is only when we 'give up and turn back' — only when we cease seeking peace and fulfilment in objective experience and turn the mind in the directionless direction, allowing it to sink deeper and deeper into the heart of awareness from which it has arisen — that we begin to taste the lasting peace and fulfilment for which have longed all our life."

— Rupert Spira,
Being Aware of Being Aware

Introduction

This journal was born from a year of falling in love with the Self. Learning to ask the sacred question, "Am I aware?" (from Rupert Spira's book *Being Aware of Being Aware*) brought such great peace, love, abundance and joy that our physical realities became permeated with the knowing that everything was happening in our favor.

Asking "Am I aware?" takes the attention away from the thought stream and sinks it squarely on the source of consciousness: awareness itself. When you genuinely ask the question and listen for the answer, your mind does a no-thought of recognizing that yes, I am aware. That knowing that you are aware is the knowing of god.

All thoughts, perceptions and experiences are made up of pure awareness. There are forms that change, and then there is the unchanging awareness that perceives it all. When you stay identified as pure awareness, you stay one with all that is: in peace, love and happiness. When you get mixed with experience and limit the pure awareness (for example, if you start caring what someone else thinks), you forget the peace that you truly are.

Revealing the peace, happiness, abundance and love that comes with being aware of being aware (focused on your sense of being, resting as "I AM", presence itself) usually takes practice. Sometimes we can't access it at all. Which is why these daily planner pages include 3 sections leading up to asking "Am I aware?" By making it a daily practice to accept what is (YES), surrender the illusion of control (MY INTUITION SAYS), practice the feeling of gratitude (THANK YOU), and simply identity as pure awareness (AM I AWARE?), you dissolve your mind into the infinite, freeing yourself from psychological suffering while the things you want come to you.

"'Am I aware?' is a sacred
question that invites the mind
in an objectless direction.

As the mind proceeds in this
objectless direction it begins
to relax, sink or fall back
into the source of awareness
from which it has arisen.
The mind progressively loses
its colour or activity until its
essence of pure awareness
is revealed."

—Rupert Spira
Being Aware of Being Aware

A Note on the title *To Whom Is This Journal Arising?*

"The mind will subside only by means of the enquiry 'Who am I?' The thought 'Who am I?', destroying all other thoughts, will itself finally be destroyed like the stick used for stirring the funeral pyre. If other thoughts rise one should, without attempting to complete them, enquire 'To whom did they rise?' What does it matter however many thoughts rise? At the very moment that each thought rises, if one vigilantly enquires 'To whom did this rise?', it will be known 'To me'. If one then enquires 'Who am I?', the mind will turn back to its source [the Self] and the thought which had risen will also subside. By repeatedly practising thus, the power of the mind to abide in its source increases."

—Sri Ramana Maharshi

This book was created after practicing Rupert Spira's "Am I aware?" question, but one of Spira's primary influences was Sri Ramana Maharshi. Maharshi taught a similar sacred question to dissolve the mind into the infinite: "Who am I?" The title of this journal invites its reader to turn their mind back to its source, which is also the goal of every exercise contained within.

"If you make human company too important, you will not discover your true self. Relationships not based in truth are never entirely reliable and are rarely enduring. Taking time to discover yourself is the best use of time. Prioritise this. One shall not excessively seek partners or friends. One should seek to know and be oneself.

As you begin to awaken to the Truth, you start noticing how well life flows by itself and how well you are cared for.

Life supports the physical, emotional, mental and spiritual needs of the one who is open to self-discovery.

Trust opens your eyes to the recognition of this. Surrender allows you to merge in your own Eternal Being."

— Mooji

Daily Planner Instructions

Like a traditional day planner, use these pages to write the date, your to-do list, the moon phase, and your daily divination reading. Then continue to the sections below.

YES

First, you say yes to what is. This practice helps you acknowledge and accept all the things you're hanging on to and resisting and seeking. "Yes, I'm anxious. Yes, I'm thinking about what's next. Yes, I'm hungry. Yes, I'm rushing. Yes, I hope work goes well today." And on and on. Showering what is with neutral attention relaxes your mind because the energy trapped in resisting and seeking is now used up by the neutral noticing.

MY INTUITION SAYS

Next, surrender the illusion of control by asking your intuition for advice instead of relying on the logical mind that only separates and creates problems. Use your non-dominant hand to answer the question, "My intuition says," and see how wise your true self really is.

THANK YOU

Practice the feeling of gratitude for all that is and all that is coming. Gratitude is a direct companion of presence, so if you practice gratitude first, presence is revealed. The only manifestation spell you ever need is "thank you", empowering you to see that everything truly is happening in your favor. List what you're grateful for that you already have, and the things you're grateful for in advance that you trust are coming. Really feel the enthusiasm that comes with a genuine "Thank you!" and the tone for your day will be set.

AM I AWARE?

After you stop fighting what is, open yourself up to infinite intelligence, and remind yourself it's all in your favor with "thank you", asking "Am I aware?" and feeling the true answer is much more accessible. When you get some space from your thoughts and focus on the simple knowing that You Are Here, life starts flowing. There is no agitation, because your mind is resting. There is no lack, because you see how you are always given the perfect thing at the perfect time. And there is no separation from those you love, because when you are identified as pure awareness, you are identified as the thing we all have in common. We all become one, and we are all in love, loving, loved.

When you are aware that you are aware, the miracles and manifestations you were once seeking come to you like moths to a flame. Ask yourself "Am I aware?" and give yourself the time and space to truly investigate the answer. You know you exist. You are now aware. You are now in the flow. And today is the best day of your life!

What Do You Want?

Even after you complete your daily journal planner page, you may still have unfulfilled desires that are causing you suffering. Turn to the appendix ***What Do You Want?*** in the back of this journal to transmute your seeking and resisting into attracting and allowing. Over the year you will gather a beautiful record of life unfolding perfectly for you.

FORTUNE MOON DAY / DATE

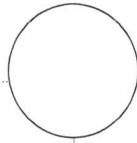

/ /

YES

MY INTUITION SAYS

THANK YOU

AM I AWARE?

FORTUNE MOON DAY / DATE

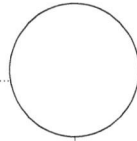

/ /

YES

MY INTUITION SAYS

THANK YOU

AM I AWARE?

DAY / DATE MOON FORTUNE

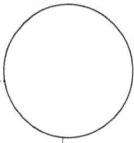

/ /

YES

MY INTUITION SAYS

THANK YOU

AM I AWARE?

DAY / DATE MOON FORTUNE

/ /

YES

MY INTUITION SAYS

THANK YOU

AM I AWARE?

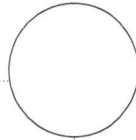

FORTUNE MOON DAY / DATE

/ /

YES

MY INTUITION SAYS

THANK YOU

AM I AWARE?

FORTUNE MOON DAY / DATE

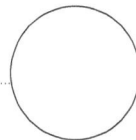

/ /

YES

MY INTUITION SAYS

THANK YOU

AM I AWARE?

DAY / DATE MOON FORTUNE

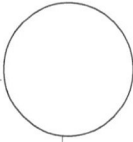

/ /

YES

MY INTUITION SAYS

THANK YOU

AM I AWARE?

DAY / DATE MOON FORTUNE

/ /

YES

MY INTUITION SAYS

THANK YOU

AM I AWARE?

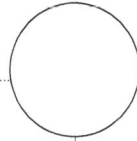

FORTUNE MOON DAY / DATE

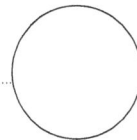

/ /

YES

MY INTUITION SAYS

THANK YOU

AM I AWARE?

FORTUNE MOON DAY / DATE

/ /

YES

MY INTUITION SAYS

THANK YOU

AM I AWARE?

DAY / DATE MOON FORTUNE

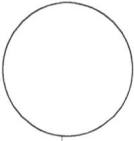

/ /

YES

MY INTUITION SAYS

THANK YOU

AM I AWARE?

DAY / DATE MOON FORTUNE

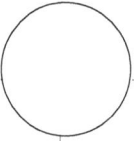

/ /

YES

MY INTUITION SAYS

THANK YOU

AM I AWARE?

FORTUNE MOON DAY / DATE

/ /

YES

MY INTUITION SAYS

THANK YOU

AM I AWARE?

FORTUNE MOON DAY / DATE

/ /

YES

MY INTUITION SAYS

THANK YOU

AM I AWARE?

DAY / DATE MOON FORTUNE

/ /

YES

MY INTUITION SAYS

THANK YOU

AM I AWARE?

DAY / DATE MOON FORTUNE

/ /

YES

MY INTUITION SAYS

THANK YOU

AM I AWARE?

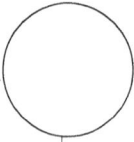

FORTUNE MOON DAY / DATE

/ /

YES

MY INTUITION SAYS

THANK YOU

AM I AWARE?

FORTUNE MOON DAY / DATE

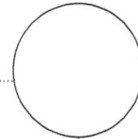

/ /

YES

MY INTUITION SAYS

THANK YOU

AM I AWARE?

DAY / DATE MOON FORTUNE

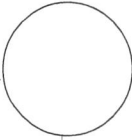

/ /

YES

MY INTUITION SAYS

THANK YOU

AM I AWARE?

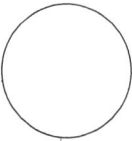

DAY / DATE MOON FORTUNE

/ /

YES

MY INTUITION SAYS

THANK YOU

AM I AWARE?

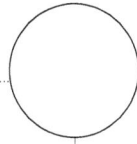

FORTUNE MOON DAY / DATE

/ /

YES

MY INTUITION SAYS

THANK YOU

AM I AWARE?

FORTUNE MOON DAY / DATE

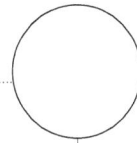

/ /

YES

MY INTUITION SAYS

THANK YOU

AM I AWARE?

DAY / DATE MOON FORTUNE

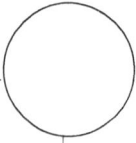

/ /

YES

MY INTUITION SAYS

THANK YOU

AM I AWARE?

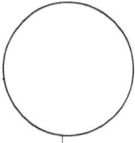

DAY / DATE MOON FORTUNE

/ /

YES

MY INTUITION SAYS

THANK YOU

AM I AWARE?

FORTUNE MOON DAY / DATE

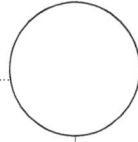

/ /

YES

MY INTUITION SAYS

THANK YOU

AM I AWARE?

FORTUNE MOON DAY / DATE

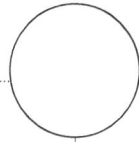

/ /

YES

MY INTUITION SAYS

THANK YOU

AM I AWARE?

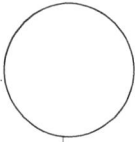

DAY / DATE MOON FORTUNE

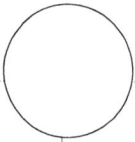

/ /

YES

MY INTUITION SAYS

THANK YOU

AM I AWARE?

DAY / DATE MOON FORTUNE

/ /

YES

MY INTUITION SAYS

THANK YOU

AM I AWARE?

FORTUNE MOON DAY / DATE

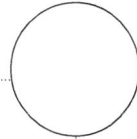

/ /

YES

MY INTUITION SAYS

THANK YOU

AM I AWARE?

FORTUNE MOON DAY / DATE

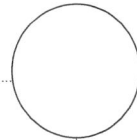

/ /

YES

MY INTUITION SAYS

THANK YOU

AM I AWARE?

DAY / DATE MOON FORTUNE

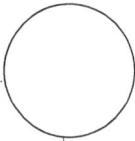

/ /

YES

MY INTUITION SAYS

THANK YOU

AM I AWARE?

DAY / DATE MOON FORTUNE

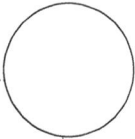

/ /

YES

MY INTUITION SAYS

THANK YOU

AM I AWARE?

FORTUNE MOON DAY / DATE

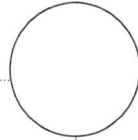

/ /

YES

MY INTUITION SAYS

THANK YOU

AM I AWARE?

FORTUNE MOON DAY / DATE

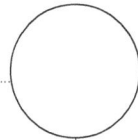

/ /

YES

MY INTUITION SAYS

THANK YOU

AM I AWARE?

DAY / DATE MOON FORTUNE

/ /

YES

MY INTUITION SAYS

THANK YOU

AM I AWARE?

DAY / DATE MOON FORTUNE

/ /

YES

MY INTUITION SAYS

THANK YOU

AM I AWARE?

FORTUNE MOON DAY / DATE

/ /

YES

MY INTUITION SAYS

THANK YOU

AM I AWARE?

FORTUNE MOON DAY / DATE

/ /

YES

MY INTUITION SAYS

THANK YOU

AM I AWARE?

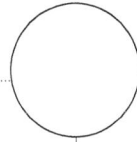

DAY / DATE MOON FORTUNE

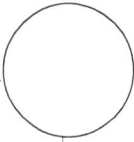

/ /

YES

MY INTUITION SAYS

THANK YOU

AM I AWARE?

DAY / DATE MOON FORTUNE

/ /

YES

MY INTUITION SAYS

THANK YOU

AM I AWARE?

FORTUNE MOON DAY / DATE

/ /

YES

MY INTUITION SAYS

THANK YOU

AM I AWARE?

FORTUNE MOON DAY / DATE

/ /

YES

MY INTUITION SAYS

THANK YOU

AM I AWARE?

DAY / DATE MOON FORTUNE

/ /

YES

MY INTUITION SAYS

THANK YOU

AM I AWARE?

DAY / DATE MOON FORTUNE

/ /

YES

MY INTUITION SAYS

THANK YOU

AM I AWARE?

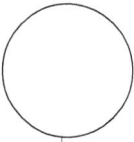

FORTUNE MOON DAY / DATE

/ /

YES

MY INTUITION SAYS

THANK YOU

AM I AWARE?

FORTUNE MOON DAY / DATE

/ /

YES

MY INTUITION SAYS

THANK YOU

AM I AWARE?

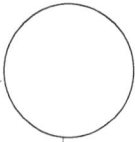

DAY / DATE MOON FORTUNE

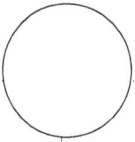

/ /

YES

MY INTUITION SAYS

THANK YOU

AM I AWARE?

DAY / DATE MOON FORTUNE

/ /

YES

MY INTUITION SAYS

THANK YOU

AM I AWARE?

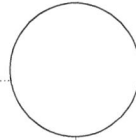

FORTUNE MOON DAY / DATE

/ /

YES

MY INTUITION SAYS

THANK YOU

AM I AWARE?

FORTUNE MOON DAY / DATE

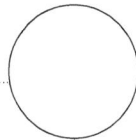

/ /

YES

MY INTUITION SAYS

THANK YOU

AM I AWARE?

DAY / DATE MOON FORTUNE

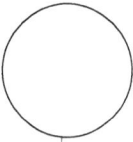

/ /

YES

MY INTUITION SAYS

THANK YOU

AM I AWARE?

DAY / DATE MOON FORTUNE

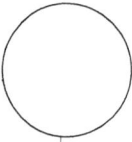

/ /

YES

MY INTUITION SAYS

THANK YOU

AM I AWARE?

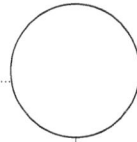

FORTUNE MOON DAY / DATE

/ /

YES

MY INTUITION SAYS

THANK YOU

AM I AWARE?

FORTUNE MOON DAY / DATE

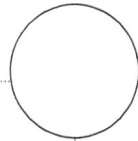

/ /

YES

MY INTUITION SAYS

THANK YOU

AM I AWARE?

DAY / DATE MOON FORTUNE

/ /

YES

MY INTUITION SAYS

THANK YOU

AM I AWARE?

DAY / DATE MOON FORTUNE

/ /

YES

MY INTUITION SAYS

THANK YOU

AM I AWARE?

FORTUNE MOON DAY / DATE

/ /

YES

MY INTUITION SAYS

THANK YOU

AM I AWARE?

FORTUNE MOON DAY / DATE

/ /

YES

MY INTUITION SAYS

THANK YOU

AM I AWARE?

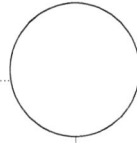

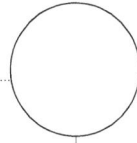

DAY / DATE MOON FORTUNE

/ /

YES

MY INTUITION SAYS

THANK YOU

AM I AWARE?

DAY / DATE MOON FORTUNE

/ /

YES

MY INTUITION SAYS

THANK YOU

AM I AWARE?

FORTUNE MOON DAY / DATE

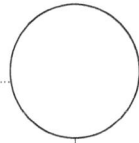

/ /

YES

MY INTUITION SAYS

THANK YOU

AM I AWARE?

FORTUNE MOON DAY / DATE

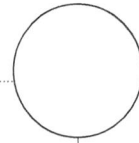

/ /

YES

MY INTUITION SAYS

THANK YOU

AM I AWARE?

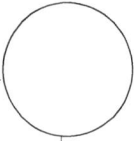

DAY / DATE MOON FORTUNE

/ /

YES

MY INTUITION SAYS

THANK YOU

AM I AWARE?

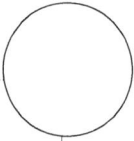

DAY / DATE MOON FORTUNE

/ /

YES

MY INTUITION SAYS

THANK YOU

AM I AWARE?

FORTUNE MOON DAY / DATE

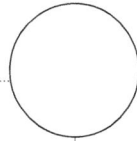

/ /

YES

MY INTUITION SAYS

THANK YOU

AM I AWARE?

FORTUNE MOON DAY / DATE

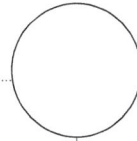

/ /

YES

MY INTUITION SAYS

THANK YOU

AM I AWARE?

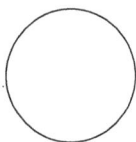

DAY / DATE MOON FORTUNE

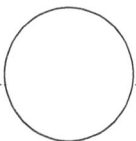

/ /

YES

MY INTUITION SAYS

THANK YOU

AM I AWARE?

DAY / DATE MOON FORTUNE

/ /

YES

MY INTUITION SAYS

THANK YOU

AM I AWARE?

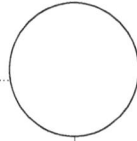

FORTUNE MOON DAY / DATE

/ /

YES

MY INTUITION SAYS

THANK YOU

AM I AWARE?

FORTUNE MOON DAY / DATE

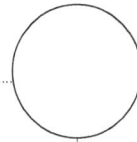

/ /

YES

MY INTUITION SAYS

THANK YOU

AM I AWARE?

DAY / DATE MOON FORTUNE

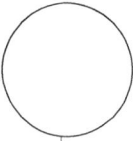

/ /

YES

MY INTUITION SAYS

THANK YOU

AM I AWARE?

DAY / DATE MOON FORTUNE

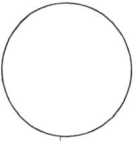

/ /

YES

MY INTUITION SAYS

THANK YOU

AM I AWARE?

FORTUNE MOON DAY / DATE

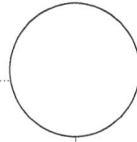

/ /

YES

MY INTUITION SAYS

THANK YOU

AM I AWARE?

FORTUNE MOON DAY / DATE

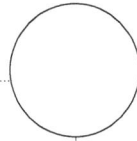

/ /

YES

MY INTUITION SAYS

THANK YOU

AM I AWARE?

DAY / DATE MOON FORTUNE

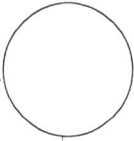

/ /

YES

MY INTUITION SAYS

THANK YOU

AM I AWARE?

DAY / DATE MOON FORTUNE

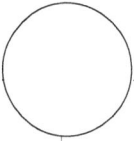

/ /

YES

MY INTUITION SAYS

THANK YOU

AM I AWARE?

FORTUNE MOON DAY / DATE

/ /

YES

MY INTUITION SAYS

THANK YOU

AM I AWARE?

FORTUNE MOON DAY / DATE

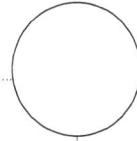

/ /

YES

MY INTUITION SAYS

THANK YOU

AM I AWARE?

DAY / DATE MOON FORTUNE

/ /

YES

MY INTUITION SAYS

THANK YOU

AM I AWARE?

DAY / DATE MOON FORTUNE

/ /

YES

MY INTUITION SAYS

THANK YOU

AM I AWARE?

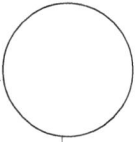

FORTUNE MOON DAY / DATE

/ /

YES

MY INTUITION SAYS

THANK YOU

AM I AWARE?

FORTUNE MOON DAY / DATE

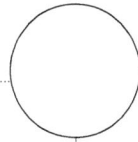

/ /

YES

MY INTUITION SAYS

THANK YOU

AM I AWARE?

DAY / DATE MOON FORTUNE

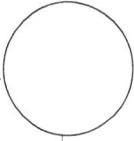

/ /

YES

MY INTUITION SAYS

THANK YOU

AM I AWARE?

DAY / DATE MOON FORTUNE

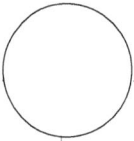

/ /

YES

MY INTUITION SAYS

THANK YOU

AM I AWARE?

FORTUNE MOON DAY / DATE

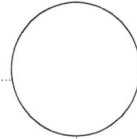

/ /

YES

MY INTUITION SAYS

THANK YOU

AM I AWARE?

FORTUNE MOON DAY / DATE

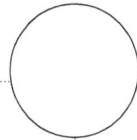

/ /

YES

MY INTUITION SAYS

THANK YOU

AM I AWARE?

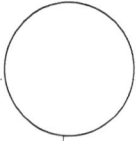

DAY / DATE MOON FORTUNE

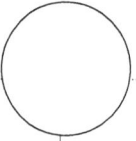

/ /

YES

MY INTUITION SAYS

THANK YOU

AM I AWARE?

DAY / DATE MOON FORTUNE

/ /

YES

MY INTUITION SAYS

THANK YOU

AM I AWARE?

FORTUNE MOON DAY / DATE

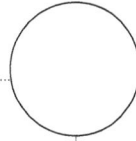

/ /

YES

MY INTUITION SAYS

THANK YOU

AM I AWARE?

FORTUNE MOON DAY / DATE

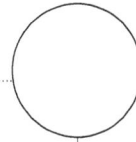

/ /

YES

MY INTUITION SAYS

THANK YOU

AM I AWARE?

DAY / DATE MOON FORTUNE

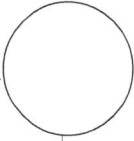

/ /

YES

MY INTUITION SAYS

THANK YOU

AM I AWARE?

DAY / DATE MOON FORTUNE

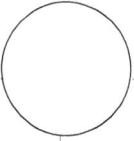

/ /

YES

MY INTUITION SAYS

THANK YOU

AM I AWARE?

FORTUNE MOON DAY / DATE

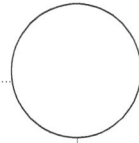

/ /

YES

MY INTUITION SAYS

THANK YOU

AM I AWARE?

FORTUNE MOON DAY / DATE

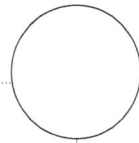

/ /

YES

MY INTUITION SAYS

THANK YOU

AM I AWARE?

DAY / DATE MOON FORTUNE

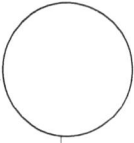

/ /

YES

MY INTUITION SAYS

THANK YOU

AM I AWARE?

DAY / DATE MOON FORTUNE

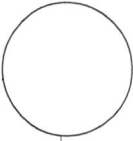

/ /

YES

MY INTUITION SAYS

THANK YOU

AM I AWARE?

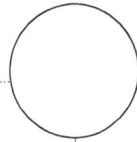

FORTUNE MOON DAY / DATE

/ /

YES

MY INTUITION SAYS

THANK YOU

AM I AWARE?

FORTUNE MOON DAY / DATE

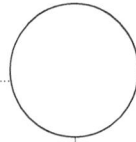

/ /

YES

MY INTUITION SAYS

THANK YOU

AM I AWARE?

DAY / DATE MOON FORTUNE

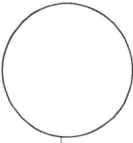

/ /

YES

MY INTUITION SAYS

THANK YOU

AM I AWARE?

DAY / DATE MOON FORTUNE

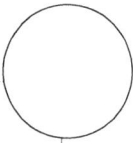

/ /

YES

MY INTUITION SAYS

THANK YOU

AM I AWARE?

FORTUNE MOON DAY / DATE

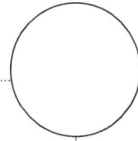

/ /

YES

MY INTUITION SAYS

THANK YOU

AM I AWARE?

FORTUNE MOON DAY / DATE

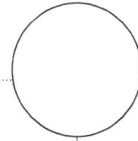

/ /

YES

MY INTUITION SAYS

THANK YOU

AM I AWARE?

DAY / DATE MOON FORTUNE

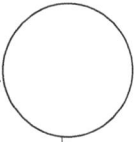

/ /

YES

MY INTUITION SAYS

THANK YOU

AM I AWARE?

DAY / DATE MOON FORTUNE

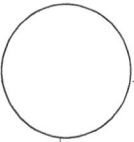

/ /

YES

MY INTUITION SAYS

THANK YOU

AM I AWARE?

FORTUNE MOON DAY / DATE

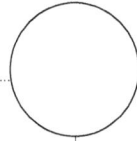

/ /

YES

MY INTUITION SAYS

THANK YOU

AM I AWARE?

FORTUNE MOON DAY / DATE

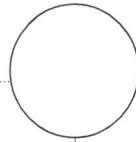

/ /

YES

MY INTUITION SAYS

THANK YOU

AM I AWARE?

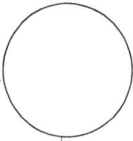

DAY / DATE MOON FORTUNE

/ /

YES

MY INTUITION SAYS

THANK YOU

AM I AWARE?

DAY / DATE MOON FORTUNE

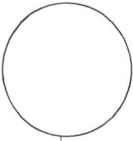

/ /

YES

MY INTUITION SAYS

THANK YOU

AM I AWARE?

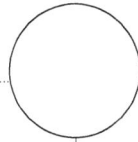

FORTUNE MOON DAY / DATE

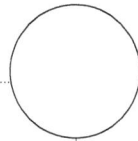

/ /

YES

MY INTUITION SAYS

THANK YOU

AM I AWARE?

FORTUNE MOON DAY / DATE

/ /

YES

MY INTUITION SAYS

THANK YOU

AM I AWARE?

DAY / DATE MOON FORTUNE

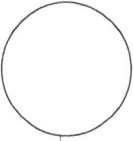

/ /

YES

MY INTUITION SAYS

THANK YOU

AM I AWARE?

DAY / DATE MOON FORTUNE

/ /

YES

MY INTUITION SAYS

THANK YOU

AM I AWARE?

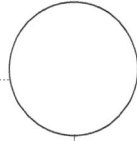

FORTUNE MOON DAY / DATE

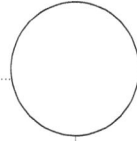

/ /

YES

MY INTUITION SAYS

THANK YOU

AM I AWARE?

FORTUNE MOON DAY / DATE

/ /

YES

MY INTUITION SAYS

THANK YOU

AM I AWARE?

DAY / DATE MOON FORTUNE

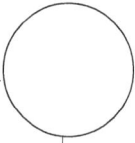

/ /

YES

MY INTUITION SAYS

THANK YOU

AM I AWARE?

DAY / DATE MOON FORTUNE

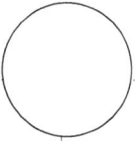

/ /

YES

MY INTUITION SAYS

THANK YOU

AM I AWARE?

FORTUNE MOON DAY / DATE

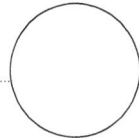

/ /

YES

MY INTUITION SAYS

THANK YOU

AM I AWARE?

FORTUNE MOON DAY / DATE

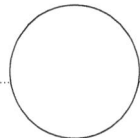

/ /

YES

MY INTUITION SAYS

THANK YOU

AM I AWARE?

DAY / DATE MOON FORTUNE

/ /

YES

MY INTUITION SAYS

THANK YOU

AM I AWARE?

DAY / DATE MOON FORTUNE

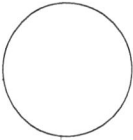

/ /

YES

MY INTUITION SAYS

THANK YOU

AM I AWARE?

FORTUNE MOON DAY / DATE

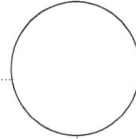

/ /

YES

MY INTUITION SAYS

THANK YOU

AM I AWARE?

FORTUNE MOON DAY / DATE

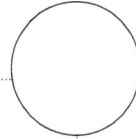

/ /

YES

MY INTUITION SAYS

THANK YOU

AM I AWARE?

DAY / DATE MOON FORTUNE

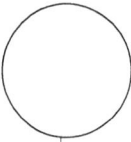

/ /

YES

MY INTUITION SAYS

THANK YOU

AM I AWARE?

DAY / DATE MOON FORTUNE

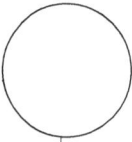

/ /

YES

MY INTUITION SAYS

THANK YOU

AM I AWARE?

FORTUNE MOON DAY / DATE

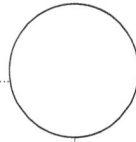

/ /

YES

MY INTUITION SAYS

THANK YOU

AM I AWARE?

FORTUNE MOON DAY / DATE

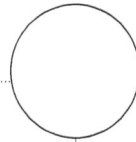

/ /

YES

MY INTUITION SAYS

THANK YOU

AM I AWARE?

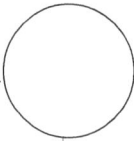

DAY / DATE MOON FORTUNE

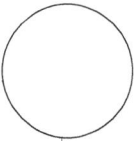

/ /

YES

MY INTUITION SAYS

THANK YOU

AM I AWARE?

DAY / DATE MOON FORTUNE

/ /

YES

MY INTUITION SAYS

THANK YOU

AM I AWARE?

FORTUNE MOON DAY / DATE

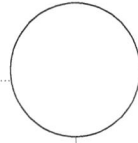

/ /

YES

MY INTUITION SAYS

THANK YOU

AM I AWARE?

FORTUNE MOON DAY / DATE

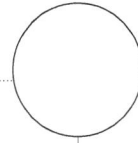

/ /

YES

MY INTUITION SAYS

THANK YOU

AM I AWARE?

DAY / DATE MOON FORTUNE

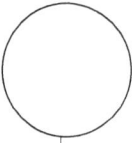

/ /

YES

MY INTUITION SAYS

THANK YOU

AM I AWARE?

DAY / DATE MOON FORTUNE

/ /

YES

MY INTUITION SAYS

THANK YOU

AM I AWARE?

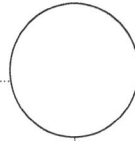

FORTUNE MOON DAY / DATE

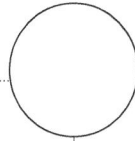

/ /

YES

MY INTUITION SAYS

THANK YOU

AM I AWARE?

FORTUNE MOON DAY / DATE

/ /

YES

MY INTUITION SAYS

THANK YOU

AM I AWARE?

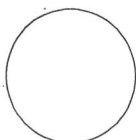

DAY / DATE MOON FORTUNE

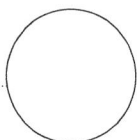

/ /

YES

MY INTUITION SAYS

THANK YOU

AM I AWARE?

DAY / DATE MOON FORTUNE

/ /

YES

MY INTUITION SAYS

THANK YOU

AM I AWARE?

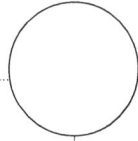

FORTUNE MOON DAY / DATE

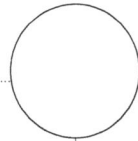

/ /

YES

MY INTUITION SAYS

THANK YOU

AM I AWARE?

FORTUNE MOON DAY / DATE

/ /

YES

MY INTUITION SAYS

THANK YOU

AM I AWARE?

DAY / DATE MOON FORTUNE

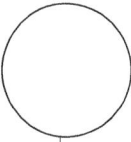

/ /

YES

MY INTUITION SAYS

THANK YOU

AM I AWARE?

DAY / DATE MOON FORTUNE

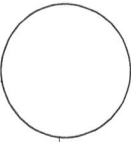

/ /

YES

MY INTUITION SAYS

THANK YOU

AM I AWARE?

FORTUNE MOON DAY / DATE

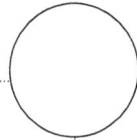

/ /

YES

MY INTUITION SAYS

THANK YOU

AM I AWARE?

FORTUNE MOON DAY / DATE

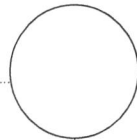

/ /

YES

MY INTUITION SAYS

THANK YOU

AM I AWARE?

DAY / DATE MOON FORTUNE

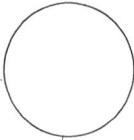

/ /

YES

MY INTUITION SAYS

THANK YOU

AM I AWARE?

DAY / DATE MOON FORTUNE

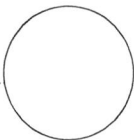

/ /

YES

MY INTUITION SAYS

THANK YOU

AM I AWARE?

FORTUNE MOON DAY / DATE

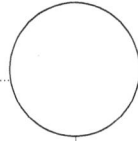

/ /

YES

MY INTUITION SAYS

THANK YOU

AM I AWARE?

FORTUNE MOON DAY / DATE

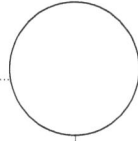

/ /

YES

MY INTUITION SAYS

THANK YOU

AM I AWARE?

DAY / DATE MOON FORTUNE

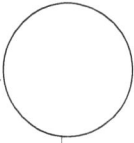

/ /

YES

MY INTUITION SAYS

THANK YOU

AM I AWARE?

DAY / DATE MOON FORTUNE

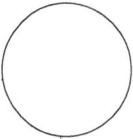

/ /

YES

MY INTUITION SAYS

THANK YOU

AM I AWARE?

FORTUNE MOON DAY / DATE

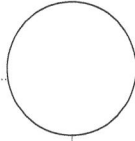

/ /

YES

MY INTUITION SAYS

THANK YOU

AM I AWARE?

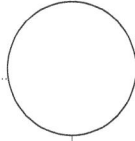

FORTUNE MOON DAY / DATE

/ /

YES

MY INTUITION SAYS

THANK YOU

AM I AWARE?

DAY / DATE MOON FORTUNE

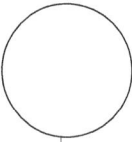

/ /

YES

MY INTUITION SAYS

THANK YOU

AM I AWARE?

DAY / DATE MOON FORTUNE

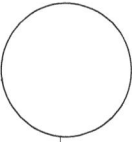

/ /

YES

MY INTUITION SAYS

THANK YOU

AM I AWARE?

FORTUNE MOON DAY / DATE

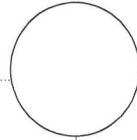

/ /

YES

MY INTUITION SAYS

THANK YOU

AM I AWARE?

FORTUNE MOON DAY / DATE

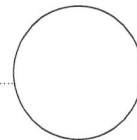

/ /

YES

MY INTUITION SAYS

THANK YOU

AM I AWARE?

DAY / DATE MOON FORTUNE

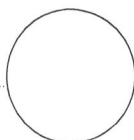

/ /

YES

MY INTUITION SAYS

THANK YOU

AM I AWARE?

DAY / DATE MOON FORTUNE

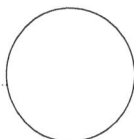

/ /

YES

MY INTUITION SAYS

THANK YOU

AM I AWARE?

FORTUNE MOON DAY / DATE

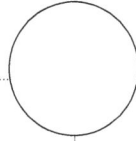

/ /

YES

MY INTUITION SAYS

THANK YOU

AM I AWARE?

FORTUNE MOON DAY / DATE

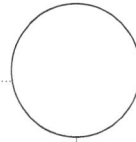

/ /

YES

MY INTUITION SAYS

THANK YOU

AM I AWARE?

DAY / DATE MOON FORTUNE

/ /

YES

MY INTUITION SAYS

THANK YOU

AM I AWARE?

DAY / DATE MOON FORTUNE

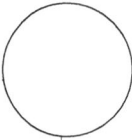

/ /

YES

MY INTUITION SAYS

THANK YOU

AM I AWARE?

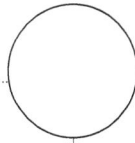

FORTUNE MOON DAY / DATE

/ /

YES

MY INTUITION SAYS

THANK YOU

AM I AWARE?

FORTUNE MOON DAY / DATE

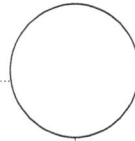

/ /

YES

MY INTUITION SAYS

THANK YOU

AM I AWARE?

DAY / DATE MOON FORTUNE

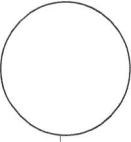

/ /

YES

MY INTUITION SAYS

THANK YOU

AM I AWARE?

DAY / DATE MOON FORTUNE

/ /

YES

MY INTUITION SAYS

THANK YOU

AM I AWARE?

FORTUNE MOON DAY / DATE

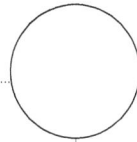

/ /

YES

MY INTUITION SAYS

THANK YOU

AM I AWARE?

FORTUNE MOON DAY / DATE

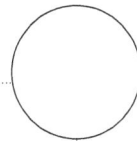

/ /

YES

MY INTUITION SAYS

THANK YOU

AM I AWARE?

DAY / DATE MOON FORTUNE

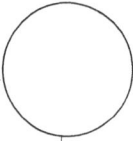

/ /

YES

MY INTUITION SAYS

THANK YOU

AM I AWARE?

DAY / DATE MOON FORTUNE

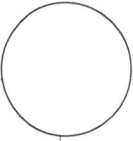

/ /

YES

MY INTUITION SAYS

THANK YOU

AM I AWARE?

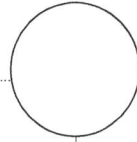

FORTUNE MOON DAY / DATE

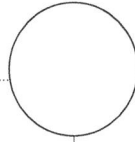

/ /

YES

MY INTUITION SAYS

THANK YOU

AM I AWARE?

FORTUNE MOON DAY / DATE

/ /

YES

MY INTUITION SAYS

THANK YOU

AM I AWARE?

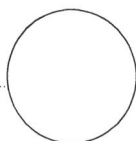

DAY / DATE MOON FORTUNE

/ /

YES

MY INTUITION SAYS

THANK YOU

AM I AWARE?

DAY / DATE MOON FORTUNE

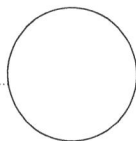

/ /

YES

MY INTUITION SAYS

THANK YOU

AM I AWARE?

FORTUNE MOON DAY / DATE

/ /

YES

MY INTUITION SAYS

THANK YOU

AM I AWARE?

FORTUNE MOON DAY / DATE

/ /

YES

MY INTUITION SAYS

THANK YOU

AM I AWARE?

DAY / DATE MOON FORTUNE

/ /

YES

MY INTUITION SAYS

THANK YOU

AM I AWARE?

DAY / DATE MOON FORTUNE

/ /

YES

MY INTUITION SAYS

THANK YOU

AM I AWARE?

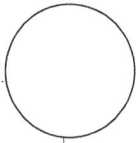

FORTUNE MOON DAY / DATE

/ /

YES

MY INTUITION SAYS

THANK YOU

AM I AWARE?

FORTUNE MOON DAY / DATE

/ /

YES

MY INTUITION SAYS

THANK YOU

AM I AWARE?

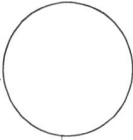

DAY / DATE MOON FORTUNE

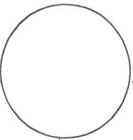

/ /

YES

MY INTUITION SAYS

THANK YOU

AM I AWARE?

DAY / DATE MOON FORTUNE

/ /

YES

MY INTUITION SAYS

THANK YOU

AM I AWARE?

FORTUNE MOON DAY / DATE

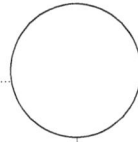

/ /

YES

MY INTUITION SAYS

THANK YOU

AM I AWARE?

FORTUNE MOON DAY / DATE

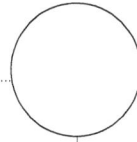

/ /

YES

MY INTUITION SAYS

THANK YOU

AM I AWARE?

DAY / DATE MOON FORTUNE

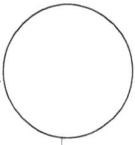

/ /

YES

MY INTUITION SAYS

THANK YOU

AM I AWARE?

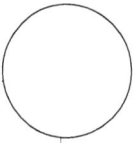

DAY / DATE MOON FORTUNE

/ /

YES

MY INTUITION SAYS

THANK YOU

AM I AWARE?

FORTUNE MOON DAY / DATE

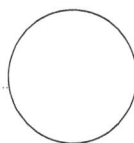

/ /

YES

MY INTUITION SAYS

THANK YOU

AM I AWARE?

FORTUNE MOON DAY / DATE

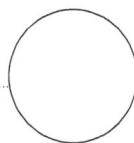

/ /

YES

MY INTUITION SAYS

THANK YOU

AM I AWARE?

DAY / DATE MOON FORTUNE

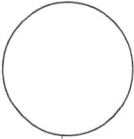

/ /

YES

MY INTUITION SAYS

THANK YOU

AM I AWARE?

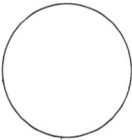

DAY / DATE MOON FORTUNE

/ /

YES

MY INTUITION SAYS

THANK YOU

AM I AWARE?

FORTUNE MOON DAY / DATE

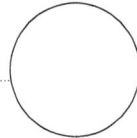

/ /

YES

MY INTUITION SAYS

THANK YOU

AM I AWARE?

FORTUNE MOON DAY / DATE

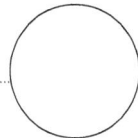

/ /

YES

MY INTUITION SAYS

THANK YOU

AM I AWARE?

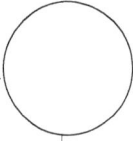

DAY / DATE MOON FORTUNE

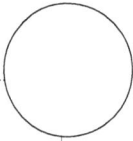

/ /

YES

MY INTUITION SAYS

THANK YOU

AM I AWARE?

DAY / DATE MOON FORTUNE

/ /

YES

MY INTUITION SAYS

THANK YOU

AM I AWARE?

FORTUNE MOON DAY / DATE

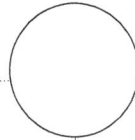

/ /

YES

MY INTUITION SAYS

THANK YOU

AM I AWARE?

FORTUNE MOON DAY / DATE

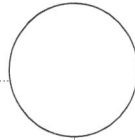

/ /

YES

MY INTUITION SAYS

THANK YOU

AM I AWARE?

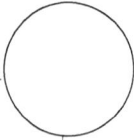

DAY / DATE MOON FORTUNE

/ /

YES

MY INTUITION SAYS

THANK YOU

AM I AWARE?

DAY / DATE MOON FORTUNE

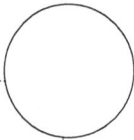

/ /

YES

MY INTUITION SAYS

THANK YOU

AM I AWARE?

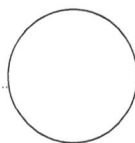

FORTUNE MOON DAY / DATE

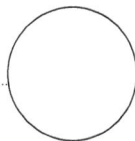

/ /

YES

MY INTUITION SAYS

THANK YOU

AM I AWARE?

FORTUNE MOON DAY / DATE

/ /

YES

MY INTUITION SAYS

THANK YOU

AM I AWARE?

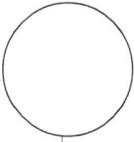

DAY / DATE MOON FORTUNE

/ /

YES

MY INTUITION SAYS

THANK YOU

AM I AWARE?

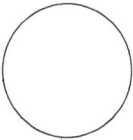

DAY / DATE MOON FORTUNE

/ /

YES

MY INTUITION SAYS

THANK YOU

AM I AWARE?

FORTUNE MOON DAY / DATE

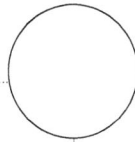

/ /

YES

MY INTUITION SAYS

THANK YOU

AM I AWARE?

FORTUNE MOON DAY / DATE

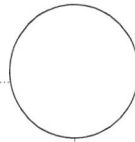

/ /

YES

MY INTUITION SAYS

THANK YOU

AM I AWARE?

DAY / DATE MOON FORTUNE

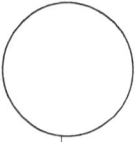

/ /

YES

MY INTUITION SAYS

THANK YOU

AM I AWARE?

DAY / DATE MOON FORTUNE

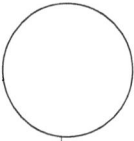

/ /

YES

MY INTUITION SAYS

THANK YOU

AM I AWARE?

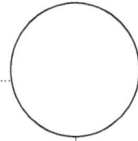

FORTUNE MOON DAY / DATE

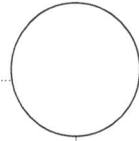

/ /

YES

MY INTUITION SAYS

THANK YOU

AM I AWARE?

FORTUNE MOON DAY / DATE

/ /

YES

MY INTUITION SAYS

THANK YOU

AM I AWARE?

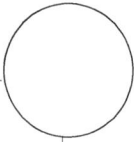

DAY / DATE MOON FORTUNE

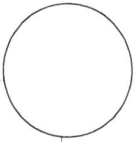

/ /

YES

MY INTUITION SAYS

THANK YOU

AM I AWARE?

DAY / DATE MOON FORTUNE

/ /

YES

MY INTUITION SAYS

THANK YOU

AM I AWARE?

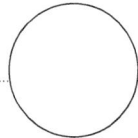

FORTUNE MOON DAY / DATE

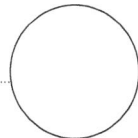

/ /

YES

MY INTUITION SAYS

THANK YOU

AM I AWARE?

FORTUNE MOON DAY / DATE

/ /

YES

MY INTUITION SAYS

THANK YOU

AM I AWARE?

DAY / DATE MOON FORTUNE

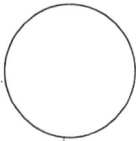

/ /

YES

MY INTUITION SAYS

THANK YOU

AM I AWARE?

DAY / DATE MOON FORTUNE

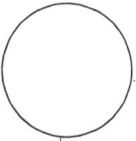

/ /

YES

MY INTUITION SAYS

THANK YOU

AM I AWARE?

FORTUNE MOON DAY / DATE

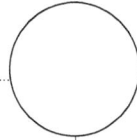

/ /

YES

MY INTUITION SAYS

THANK YOU

AM I AWARE?

FORTUNE MOON DAY / DATE

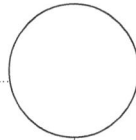

/ /

YES

MY INTUITION SAYS

THANK YOU

AM I AWARE?

DAY / DATE MOON FORTUNE

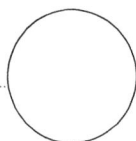

/ /

YES

MY INTUITION SAYS

THANK YOU

AM I AWARE?

DAY / DATE MOON FORTUNE

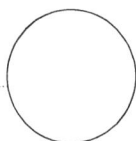

/ /

YES

MY INTUITION SAYS

THANK YOU

AM I AWARE?

FORTUNE MOON DAY / DATE

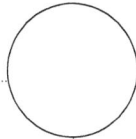

/ /

YES

MY INTUITION SAYS

THANK YOU

AM I AWARE?

FORTUNE MOON DAY / DATE

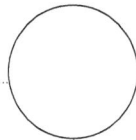

/ /

YES

MY INTUITION SAYS

THANK YOU

AM I AWARE?

DAY / DATE MOON FORTUNE

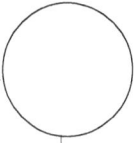

/ /

YES

MY INTUITION SAYS

THANK YOU

AM I AWARE?

DAY / DATE MOON FORTUNE

/ /

YES

MY INTUITION SAYS

THANK YOU

AM I AWARE?

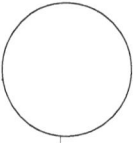

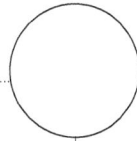

FORTUNE MOON DAY / DATE

/ /

YES

MY INTUITION SAYS

THANK YOU

AM I AWARE?

FORTUNE MOON DAY / DATE

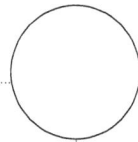

/ /

YES

MY INTUITION SAYS

THANK YOU

AM I AWARE?

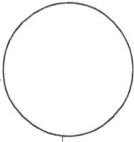

DAY / DATE MOON FORTUNE

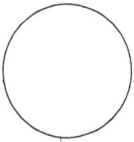

/ /

YES

MY INTUITION SAYS

THANK YOU

AM I AWARE?

DAY / DATE MOON FORTUNE

/ /

YES

MY INTUITION SAYS

THANK YOU

AM I AWARE?

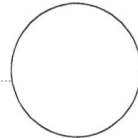

FORTUNE MOON DAY / DATE

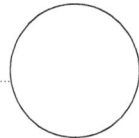

/ /

YES

MY INTUITION SAYS

THANK YOU

AM I AWARE?

FORTUNE MOON DAY / DATE

/ /

YES

MY INTUITION SAYS

THANK YOU

AM I AWARE?

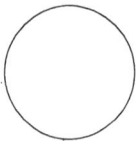

DAY / DATE MOON FORTUNE

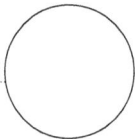

/ /

YES

MY INTUITION SAYS

THANK YOU

AM I AWARE?

DAY / DATE MOON FORTUNE

/ /

YES

MY INTUITION SAYS

THANK YOU

AM I AWARE?

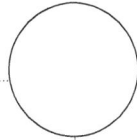

FORTUNE MOON DAY / DATE

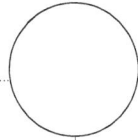

/ /

YES

MY INTUITION SAYS

THANK YOU

AM I AWARE?

FORTUNE MOON DAY / DATE

/ /

YES

MY INTUITION SAYS

THANK YOU

AM I AWARE?

DAY / DATE MOON FORTUNE

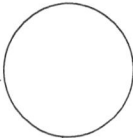

/ /

YES

MY INTUITION SAYS

THANK YOU

AM I AWARE?

DAY / DATE MOON FORTUNE

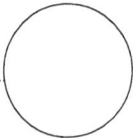

/ /

YES

MY INTUITION SAYS

THANK YOU

AM I AWARE?

FORTUNE MOON DAY / DATE

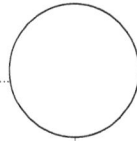

/ /

YES

MY INTUITION SAYS

THANK YOU

AM I AWARE?

FORTUNE MOON DAY / DATE

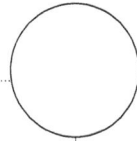

/ /

YES

MY INTUITION SAYS

THANK YOU

AM I AWARE?

DAY / DATE MOON FORTUNE

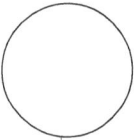

/ /

YES

MY INTUITION SAYS

THANK YOU

AM I AWARE?

DAY / DATE MOON FORTUNE

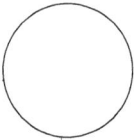

/ /

YES

MY INTUITION SAYS

THANK YOU

AM I AWARE?

FORTUNE MOON DAY / DATE

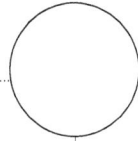

/ /

YES

MY INTUITION SAYS

THANK YOU

AM I AWARE?

FORTUNE MOON DAY / DATE

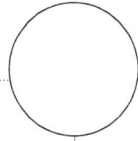

/ /

YES

MY INTUITION SAYS

THANK YOU

AM I AWARE?

DAY / DATE MOON FORTUNE

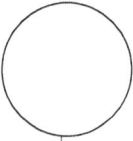

/ /

YES

MY INTUITION SAYS

THANK YOU

AM I AWARE?

DAY / DATE MOON FORTUNE

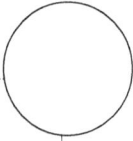

/ /

YES

MY INTUITION SAYS

THANK YOU

AM I AWARE?

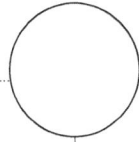

FORTUNE MOON DAY / DATE

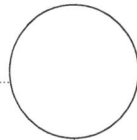

/ /

YES

MY INTUITION SAYS

THANK YOU

AM I AWARE?

FORTUNE MOON DAY / DATE

/ /

YES

MY INTUITION SAYS

THANK YOU

AM I AWARE?

DAY / DATE MOON FORTUNE

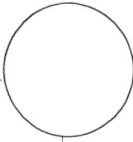

/ /

YES

MY INTUITION SAYS

THANK YOU

AM I AWARE?

DAY / DATE MOON FORTUNE

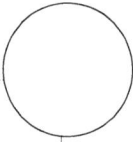

/ /

YES

MY INTUITION SAYS

THANK YOU

AM I AWARE?

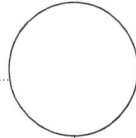

FORTUNE MOON DAY / DATE

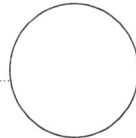

/ /

YES

MY INTUITION SAYS

THANK YOU

AM I AWARE?

FORTUNE MOON DAY / DATE

/ /

YES

MY INTUITION SAYS

THANK YOU

AM I AWARE?

DAY / DATE MOON FORTUNE

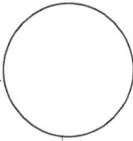

/ /

YES

MY INTUITION SAYS

THANK YOU

AM I AWARE?

DAY / DATE MOON FORTUNE

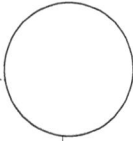

/ /

YES

MY INTUITION SAYS

THANK YOU

AM I AWARE?

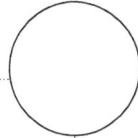

FORTUNE MOON DAY / DATE

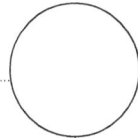

/ /

YES

MY INTUITION SAYS

THANK YOU

AM I AWARE?

FORTUNE MOON DAY / DATE

/ /

YES

MY INTUITION SAYS

THANK YOU

AM I AWARE?

DAY / DATE MOON FORTUNE

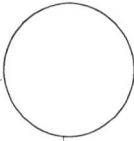

/ /

YES

MY INTUITION SAYS

THANK YOU

AM I AWARE?

DAY / DATE MOON FORTUNE

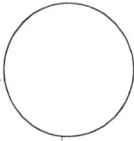

/ /

YES

MY INTUITION SAYS

THANK YOU

AM I AWARE?

FORTUNE MOON DAY / DATE

/ /

YES

MY INTUITION SAYS

THANK YOU

AM I AWARE?

FORTUNE MOON DAY / DATE

/ /

YES

MY INTUITION SAYS

THANK YOU

AM I AWARE?

DAY / DATE MOON FORTUNE

/ /

YES

MY INTUITION SAYS

THANK YOU

AM I AWARE?

DAY / DATE MOON FORTUNE

/ /

YES

MY INTUITION SAYS

THANK YOU

AM I AWARE?

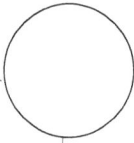

FORTUNE MOON DAY / DATE

/ /

YES

MY INTUITION SAYS

THANK YOU

AM I AWARE?

FORTUNE MOON DAY / DATE

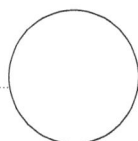

/ /

YES

MY INTUITION SAYS

THANK YOU

AM I AWARE?

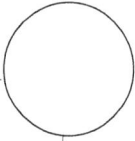

DAY / DATE MOON FORTUNE

/ /

YES

MY INTUITION SAYS

THANK YOU

AM I AWARE?

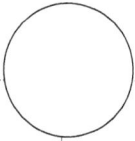

DAY / DATE MOON FORTUNE

/ /

YES

MY INTUITION SAYS

THANK YOU

AM I AWARE?

FORTUNE MOON DAY / DATE

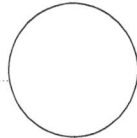

/ /

YES

MY INTUITION SAYS

THANK YOU

AM I AWARE?

FORTUNE MOON DAY / DATE

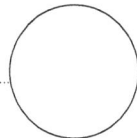

/ /

YES

MY INTUITION SAYS

THANK YOU

AM I AWARE?

DAY / DATE MOON FORTUNE

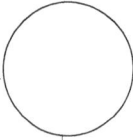

/ /

YES

MY INTUITION SAYS

THANK YOU

AM I AWARE?

DAY / DATE MOON FORTUNE

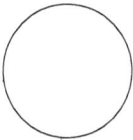

/ /

YES

MY INTUITION SAYS

THANK YOU

AM I AWARE?

FORTUNE MOON DAY / DATE

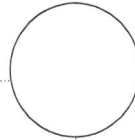

/ /

YES

MY INTUITION SAYS

THANK YOU

AM I AWARE?

FORTUNE MOON DAY / DATE

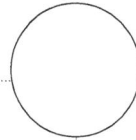

/ /

YES

MY INTUITION SAYS

THANK YOU

AM I AWARE?

DAY / DATE MOON FORTUNE

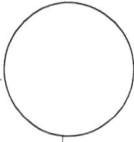

/ /

YES

MY INTUITION SAYS

THANK YOU

AM I AWARE?

DAY / DATE MOON FORTUNE

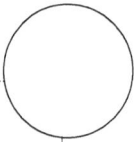

/ /

YES

MY INTUITION SAYS

THANK YOU

AM I AWARE?

FORTUNE MOON DAY / DATE

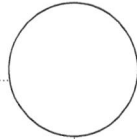

/ /

YES

MY INTUITION SAYS

THANK YOU

AM I AWARE?

FORTUNE MOON DAY / DATE

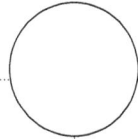

/ /

YES

MY INTUITION SAYS

THANK YOU

AM I AWARE?

DAY / DATE MOON FORTUNE

/ /

YES

MY INTUITION SAYS

THANK YOU

AM I AWARE?

DAY / DATE MOON FORTUNE

/ /

YES

MY INTUITION SAYS

THANK YOU

AM I AWARE?

FORTUNE MOON DAY / DATE

/ /

YES

MY INTUITION SAYS

THANK YOU

AM I AWARE?

FORTUNE MOON DAY / DATE

/ /

YES

MY INTUITION SAYS

THANK YOU

AM I AWARE?

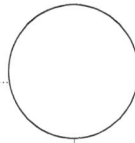

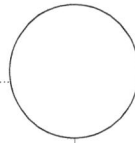

DAY / DATE MOON FORTUNE

/ /

YES

MY INTUITION SAYS

THANK YOU

AM I AWARE?

DAY / DATE MOON FORTUNE

/ /

YES

MY INTUITION SAYS

THANK YOU

AM I AWARE?

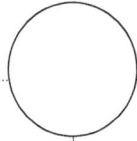

FORTUNE MOON DAY / DATE

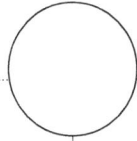

/ /

YES

MY INTUITION SAYS

THANK YOU

AM I AWARE?

FORTUNE MOON DAY / DATE

/ /

YES

MY INTUITION SAYS

THANK YOU

AM I AWARE?

DAY / DATE MOON FORTUNE

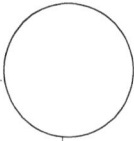

/ /

YES

MY INTUITION SAYS

THANK YOU

AM I AWARE?

DAY / DATE MOON FORTUNE

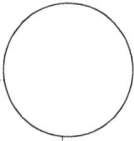

/ /

YES

MY INTUITION SAYS

THANK YOU

AM I AWARE?

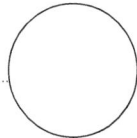

FORTUNE MOON DAY / DATE

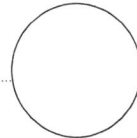

/ /

YES

MY INTUITION SAYS

THANK YOU

AM I AWARE?

FORTUNE MOON DAY / DATE

/ /

YES

MY INTUITION SAYS

THANK YOU

AM I AWARE?

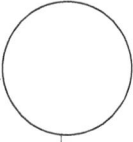

DAY / DATE MOON FORTUNE

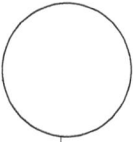

/ /

YES

MY INTUITION SAYS

THANK YOU

AM I AWARE?

DAY / DATE MOON FORTUNE

/ /

YES

MY INTUITION SAYS

THANK YOU

AM I AWARE?

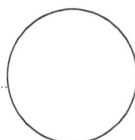

FORTUNE MOON DAY / DATE

/ /

YES

MY INTUITION SAYS

THANK YOU

AM I AWARE?

FORTUNE MOON DAY / DATE

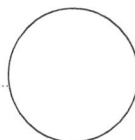

/ /

YES

MY INTUITION SAYS

THANK YOU

AM I AWARE?

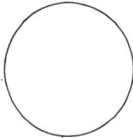

DAY / DATE MOON FORTUNE

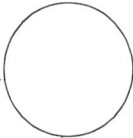

/ /

YES

MY INTUITION SAYS

THANK YOU

AM I AWARE?

DAY / DATE MOON FORTUNE

/ /

YES

MY INTUITION SAYS

THANK YOU

AM I AWARE?

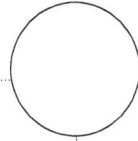

FORTUNE MOON DAY / DATE

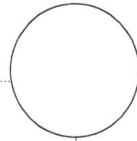

/ /

YES

MY INTUITION SAYS

THANK YOU

AM I AWARE?

FORTUNE MOON DAY / DATE

/ /

YES

MY INTUITION SAYS

THANK YOU

AM I AWARE?

DAY / DATE MOON FORTUNE

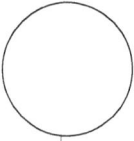

/ /

YES

MY INTUITION SAYS

THANK YOU

AM I AWARE?

DAY / DATE MOON FORTUNE

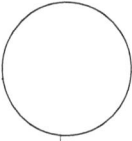

/ /

YES

MY INTUITION SAYS

THANK YOU

AM I AWARE?

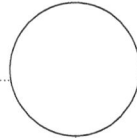

FORTUNE MOON DAY / DATE

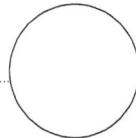

/ /

YES

MY INTUITION SAYS

THANK YOU

AM I AWARE?

FORTUNE MOON DAY / DATE

/ /

YES

MY INTUITION SAYS

THANK YOU

AM I AWARE?

DAY / DATE MOON FORTUNE

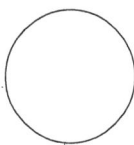

/ /

YES

MY INTUITION SAYS

THANK YOU

AM I AWARE?

DAY / DATE MOON FORTUNE

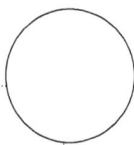

/ /

YES

MY INTUITION SAYS

THANK YOU

AM I AWARE?

FORTUNE MOON DAY / DATE

/ /

YES

MY INTUITION SAYS

THANK YOU

AM I AWARE?

FORTUNE MOON DAY / DATE

/ /

YES

MY INTUITION SAYS

THANK YOU

AM I AWARE?

DAY / DATE MOON FORTUNE

/ /

YES

MY INTUITION SAYS

THANK YOU

AM I AWARE?

DAY / DATE MOON FORTUNE

/ /

YES

MY INTUITION SAYS

THANK YOU

AM I AWARE?

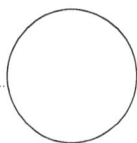

FORTUNE MOON DAY / DATE

/ /

YES

MY INTUITION SAYS

THANK YOU

AM I AWARE?

FORTUNE MOON DAY / DATE

/ /

YES

MY INTUITION SAYS

THANK YOU

AM I AWARE?

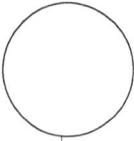

DAY / DATE MOON FORTUNE

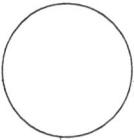

/ /

YES

MY INTUITION SAYS

THANK YOU

AM I AWARE?

DAY / DATE MOON FORTUNE

/ /

YES

MY INTUITION SAYS

THANK YOU

AM I AWARE?

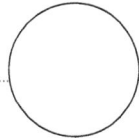

FORTUNE MOON DAY / DATE

/ /

YES

MY INTUITION SAYS

THANK YOU

AM I AWARE?

FORTUNE MOON DAY / DATE

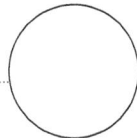

/ /

YES

MY INTUITION SAYS

THANK YOU

AM I AWARE?

DAY / DATE MOON FORTUNE

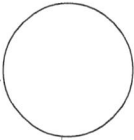

/ /

YES

MY INTUITION SAYS

THANK YOU

AM I AWARE?

DAY / DATE MOON FORTUNE

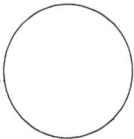

/ /

YES

MY INTUITION SAYS

THANK YOU

AM I AWARE?

FORTUNE MOON DAY / DATE

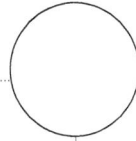

/ /

YES

MY INTUITION SAYS

THANK YOU

AM I AWARE?

FORTUNE MOON DAY / DATE

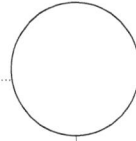

/ /

YES

MY INTUITION SAYS

THANK YOU

AM I AWARE?

DAY / DATE MOON FORTUNE

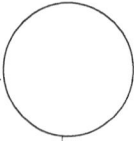

/ /

YES

MY INTUITION SAYS

THANK YOU

AM I AWARE?

DAY / DATE MOON FORTUNE

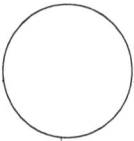

/ /

YES

MY INTUITION SAYS

THANK YOU

AM I AWARE?

FORTUNE MOON DAY / DATE

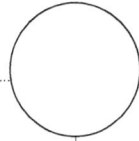

/ /

YES

MY INTUITION SAYS

THANK YOU

AM I AWARE?

FORTUNE MOON DAY / DATE

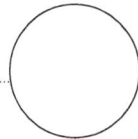

/ /

YES

MY INTUITION SAYS

THANK YOU

AM I AWARE?

DAY / DATE MOON FORTUNE

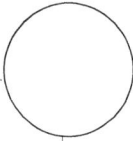

/ /

YES

MY INTUITION SAYS

THANK YOU

AM I AWARE?

DAY / DATE MOON FORTUNE

/ /

YES

MY INTUITION SAYS

THANK YOU

AM I AWARE?

FORTUNE MOON DAY / DATE

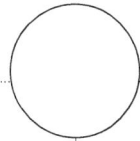

/ /

YES

MY INTUITION SAYS

THANK YOU

AM I AWARE?

FORTUNE MOON DAY / DATE

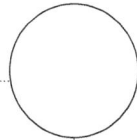

/ /

YES

MY INTUITION SAYS

THANK YOU

AM I AWARE?

DAY / DATE MOON FORTUNE

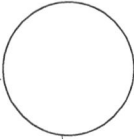

/ /

YES

MY INTUITION SAYS

THANK YOU

AM I AWARE?

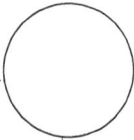

DAY / DATE MOON FORTUNE

/ /

YES

MY INTUITION SAYS

THANK YOU

AM I AWARE?

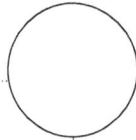

FORTUNE MOON DAY / DATE

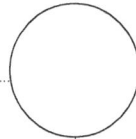

/ /

YES

MY INTUITION SAYS

THANK YOU

AM I AWARE?

FORTUNE MOON DAY / DATE

/ /

YES

MY INTUITION SAYS

THANK YOU

AM I AWARE?

DAY / DATE MOON FORTUNE

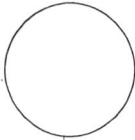

/ /

YES

MY INTUITION SAYS

THANK YOU

AM I AWARE?

DAY / DATE MOON FORTUNE

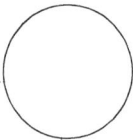

/ /

YES

MY INTUITION SAYS

THANK YOU

AM I AWARE?

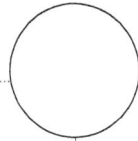

FORTUNE MOON DAY / DATE

/ /

YES

MY INTUITION SAYS

THANK YOU

AM I AWARE?

FORTUNE MOON DAY / DATE

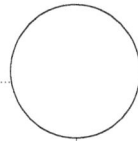

/ /

YES

MY INTUITION SAYS

THANK YOU

AM I AWARE?

DAY / DATE MOON FORTUNE

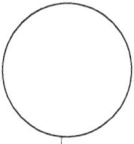

/ /

YES

MY INTUITION SAYS

THANK YOU

AM I AWARE?

DAY / DATE MOON FORTUNE

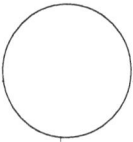

/ /

YES

MY INTUITION SAYS

THANK YOU

AM I AWARE?

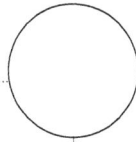

FORTUNE MOON DAY / DATE

/ /

YES

MY INTUITION SAYS

THANK YOU

AM I AWARE?

FORTUNE MOON DAY / DATE

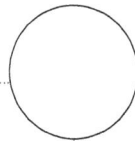

/ /

YES

MY INTUITION SAYS

THANK YOU

AM I AWARE?

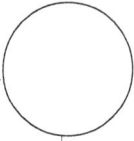

DAY / DATE MOON FORTUNE

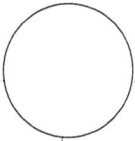

/ /

YES

MY INTUITION SAYS

THANK YOU

AM I AWARE?

DAY / DATE MOON FORTUNE

/ /

YES

MY INTUITION SAYS

THANK YOU

AM I AWARE?

FORTUNE MOON DAY / DATE

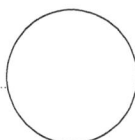

/ /

YES

MY INTUITION SAYS

THANK YOU

AM I AWARE?

FORTUNE MOON DAY / DATE

/ /

YES

MY INTUITION SAYS

THANK YOU

AM I AWARE?

DAY / DATE MOON FORTUNE

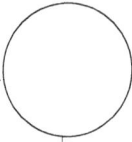

/ /

YES

MY INTUITION SAYS

THANK YOU

AM I AWARE?

DAY / DATE MOON FORTUNE

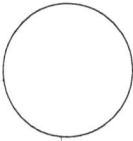

/ /

YES

MY INTUITION SAYS

THANK YOU

AM I AWARE?

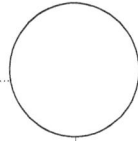

FORTUNE MOON DAY / DATE

/ /

YES

MY INTUITION SAYS

THANK YOU

AM I AWARE?

FORTUNE MOON DAY / DATE

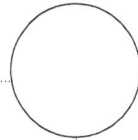

/ /

YES

MY INTUITION SAYS

THANK YOU

AM I AWARE?

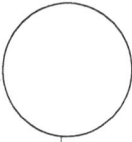

DAY / DATE MOON FORTUNE

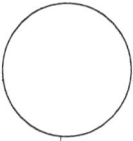

/ /

YES

MY INTUITION SAYS

THANK YOU

AM I AWARE?

DAY / DATE MOON FORTUNE

/ /

YES

MY INTUITION SAYS

THANK YOU

AM I AWARE?

FORTUNE MOON DAY / DATE

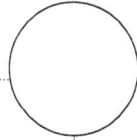

/ /

YES

MY INTUITION SAYS

THANK YOU

AM I AWARE?

FORTUNE MOON DAY / DATE

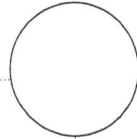

/ /

YES

MY INTUITION SAYS

THANK YOU

AM I AWARE?

DAY / DATE MOON FORTUNE

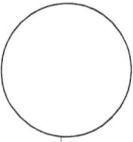

/ /

YES

MY INTUITION SAYS

THANK YOU

AM I AWARE?

DAY / DATE MOON FORTUNE

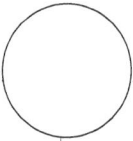

/ /

YES

MY INTUITION SAYS

THANK YOU

AM I AWARE?

FORTUNE MOON DAY / DATE

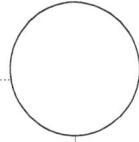

/ /

YES

MY INTUITION SAYS

THANK YOU

AM I AWARE?

FORTUNE MOON DAY / DATE

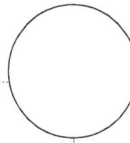

/ /

YES

MY INTUITION SAYS

THANK YOU

AM I AWARE?

DAY / DATE MOON FORTUNE

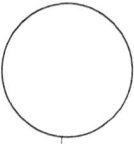

/ /

YES

MY INTUITION SAYS

THANK YOU

AM I AWARE?

DAY / DATE MOON FORTUNE

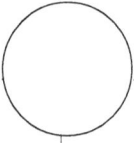

/ /

YES

MY INTUITION SAYS

THANK YOU

AM I AWARE?

FORTUNE MOON DAY / DATE

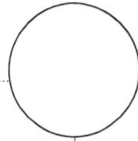

/ /

YES

MY INTUITION SAYS

THANK YOU

AM I AWARE?

FORTUNE MOON DAY / DATE

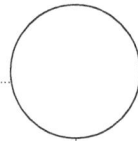

/ /

YES

MY INTUITION SAYS

THANK YOU

AM I AWARE?

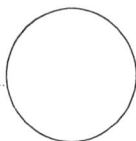

DAY / DATE MOON FORTUNE

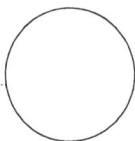

/ /

YES

MY INTUITION SAYS

THANK YOU

AM I AWARE?

DAY / DATE MOON FORTUNE

/ /

YES

MY INTUITION SAYS

THANK YOU

AM I AWARE?

FORTUNE MOON DAY / DATE

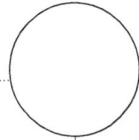

/ /

YES

MY INTUITION SAYS

THANK YOU

AM I AWARE?

FORTUNE MOON DAY / DATE

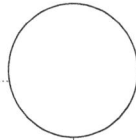

/ /

YES

MY INTUITION SAYS

THANK YOU

AM I AWARE?

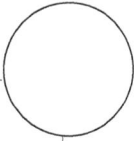

DAY / DATE MOON FORTUNE

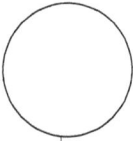

/ /

YES

MY INTUITION SAYS

THANK YOU

AM I AWARE?

DAY / DATE MOON FORTUNE

/ /

YES

MY INTUITION SAYS

THANK YOU

AM I AWARE?

FORTUNE MOON DAY / DATE

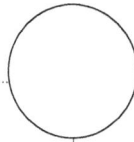

/ /

YES

MY INTUITION SAYS

THANK YOU

AM I AWARE?

FORTUNE MOON DAY / DATE

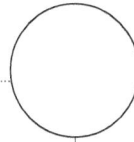

/ /

YES

MY INTUITION SAYS

THANK YOU

AM I AWARE?

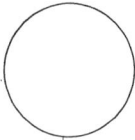

DAY / DATE MOON FORTUNE

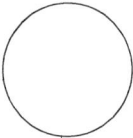

/ /

YES

MY INTUITION SAYS

THANK YOU

AM I AWARE?

DAY / DATE MOON FORTUNE

/ /

YES

MY INTUITION SAYS

THANK YOU

AM I AWARE?

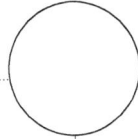

FORTUNE MOON DAY / DATE

/ /

YES

MY INTUITION SAYS

THANK YOU

AM I AWARE?

FORTUNE MOON DAY / DATE

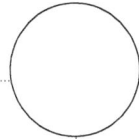

/ /

YES

MY INTUITION SAYS

THANK YOU

AM I AWARE?

What Do You Want?

Some days you need a little more help centering or connecting with your infinite self. On those days, consult this appendix for exercises specifically tailored to how you feel. Each exercise will help you build trust in the process of life, transmute seeking into manifesting power, or stabilize as the presence of god. You can complete as many as you need to feel better.

I don't want this

"Life cannot be against you, for you are life itself. Life can only seem to go against ego's projections, which are rarely in harmony with the truth."

—Mooji

Trust Exercise

Learning to surrender the separate self involves building trust in life. When life seems to be happening *to you* instead of *through you,* it's easy to get distracted into trying to control outcomes or imprisoned by strong preferences. When you notice your energy contracting in this manner, take interest.

Write down what you *think* is working against you and the date. Decide to trust the process of life and don't try to take any action. When you realize why it was actually happening in your favor, return to this page to note why. Over time, you will find it's all unfolding perfectly and you can rest in your natural state of knowing.

DATE	I thought this was happening against me	But it was happening in my favor because	DATE

DATE	I thought this was happening against me	But it was happening in my favor because	DATE

DATE	I thought this was happening against me	But it was happening in my favor because	DATE

DATE	I thought this was happening against me	But it was happening in my favor because	DATE

DATE	I thought this was happening against me	But it was happening in my favor because	DATE

Thanks Exercise

Sometimes surrendering is easier said than done. While the *Trust Exercise* helps you flex your letting go muscle, the *Thanks Exercise* helps you exercise your mental agility. Pivoting your perspective from "I don't want this" to "Maybe this change is good" can turn an unexpected intrusion into the best thing that's ever happened to you.

When you notice an annoyance or inconvenience in your life that's beyond your control to stop, imagine saying "Thanks!" to the situation at hand and write it on the card. It can be sarcastically at first, but say it. You have to admit that if you can't yet surrender completely, looking for ways to appreciate what's happening is less painful than resisting it. With enough repetition, saying thanks turns the circumstance into something to truly be grateful for. Write the good things that came on the lines at the bottom of the card.

Thanks, ______________________________

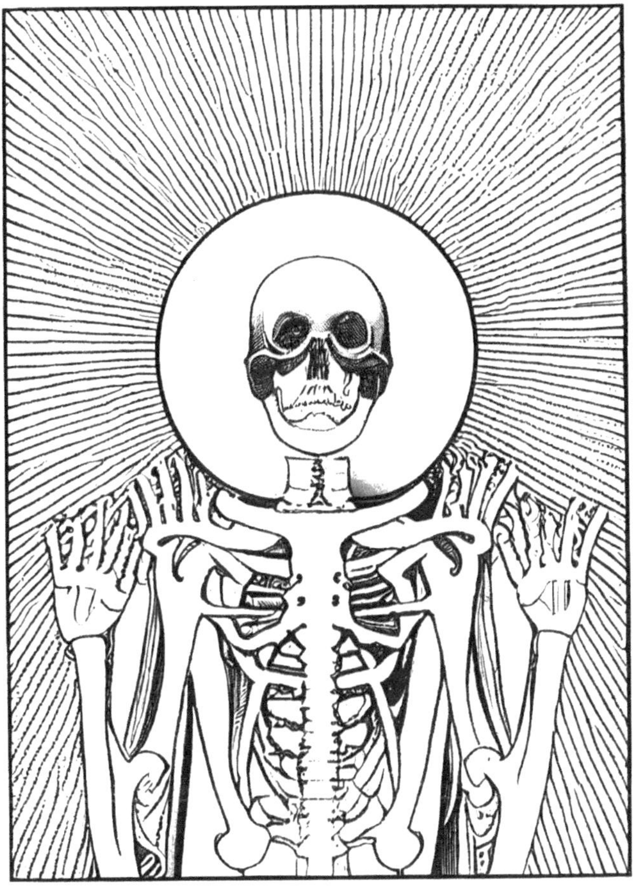

Thanks, ____________________

Thanks, ____________________

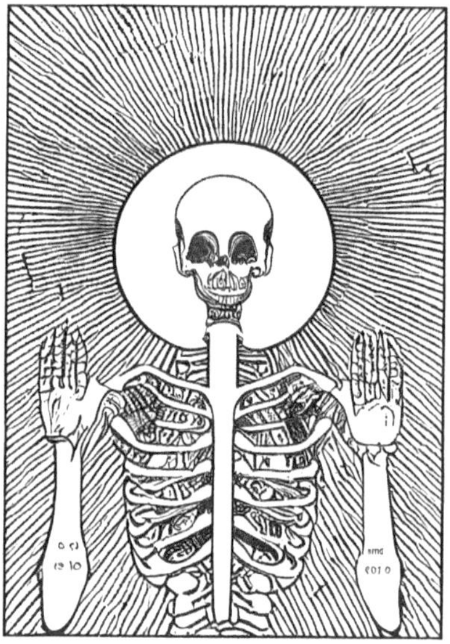

Thanks, ____________________

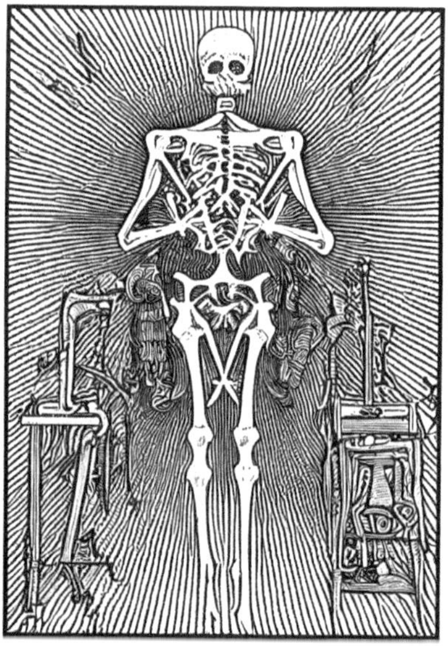

Thanks, ____________________

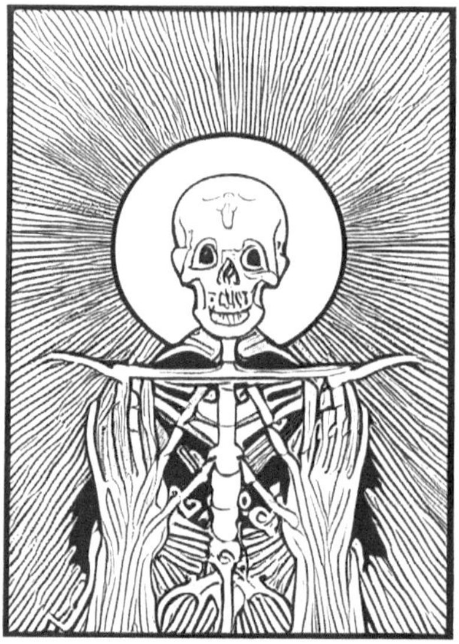

Thanks,

Thanks,

Thanks,

Thanks,

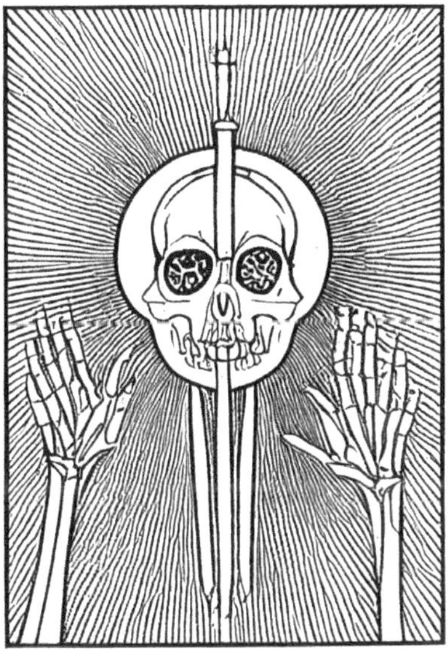

Thanks, ______________________

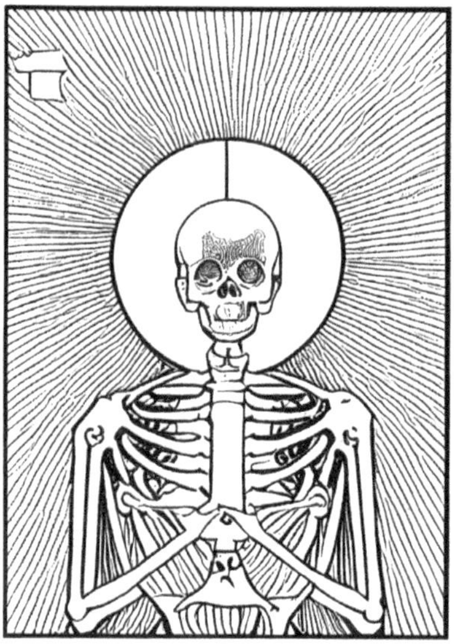

Thanks, ______________________

Thanks, ______________________

Thanks, ______________________

Thanks,

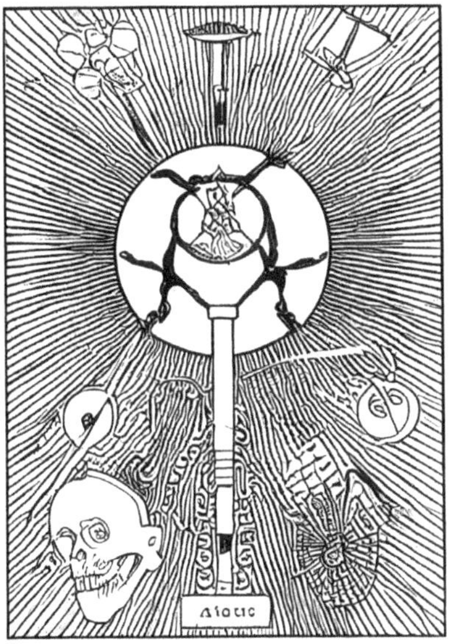

Thanks,

Thanks,

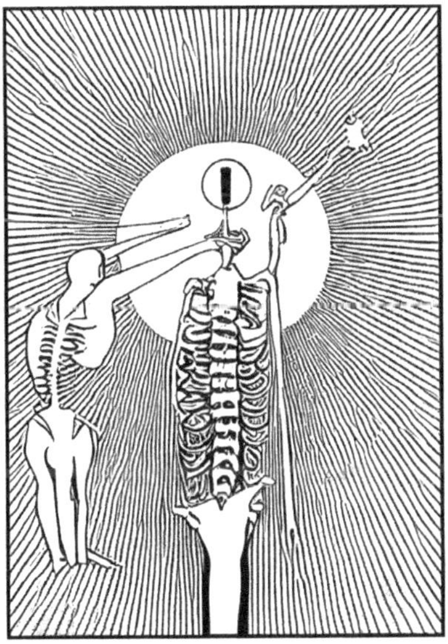

Thanks,

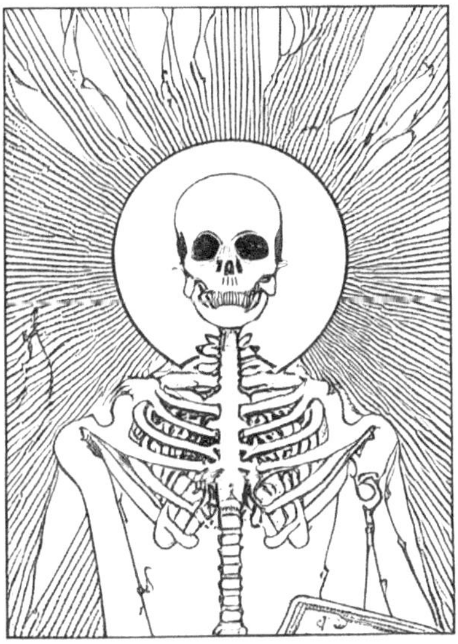

How Can I Still Feel Good If I Have to Spend the Rest of My Life ______?

Have you ever persevered through something and come out on the other side? Have you ever had a crush that you eventually got over? Have you ever had a financially rough patch or persistent health problem? How did you cope? Tap into that energy for this activity. When the contrast of your life overwhelmed you in the past, you found stores of energy to get you through.

What is the situation you're resisting? Name it in the memo provided. What if this situation persists for the rest of your life? How will you find a way to enjoy life anyway? Tap into your stardust energy and listen for the message space sends in reply.

How Can I Still Feel Good If I Have to Spend the Rest of My Life ....?

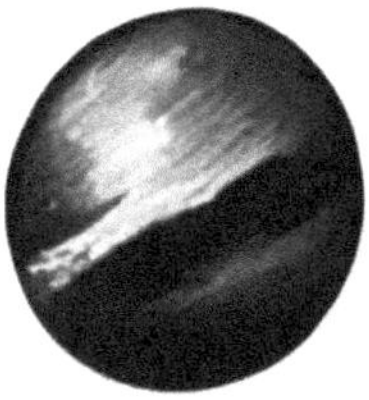

How Can I Still Feel Good If I Have to Spend the Rest of My Life ....?

How Can I Still Feel Good If I Have to Spend the Rest of My Life ....?

How Can I Still Feel Good If I Have to Spend the Rest of My Life ....?

How Can I Still Feel Good If I Have to Spend the Rest of My Life ....?

How Can I Still Feel Good
If I Have to Spend the Rest
of My Life ?

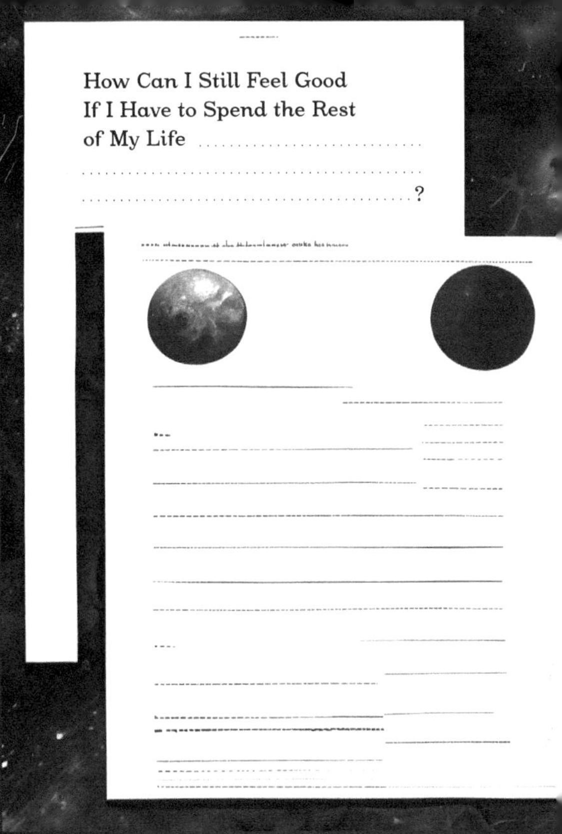
How Can I Still Feel Good
If I Have to Spend the Rest
of My Life ?

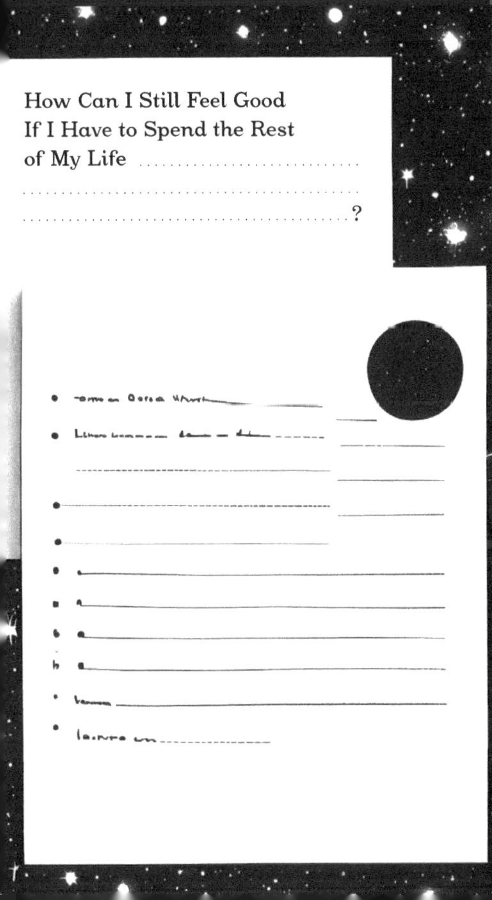
How Can I Still Feel Good
If I Have to Spend the Rest
of My Life ?

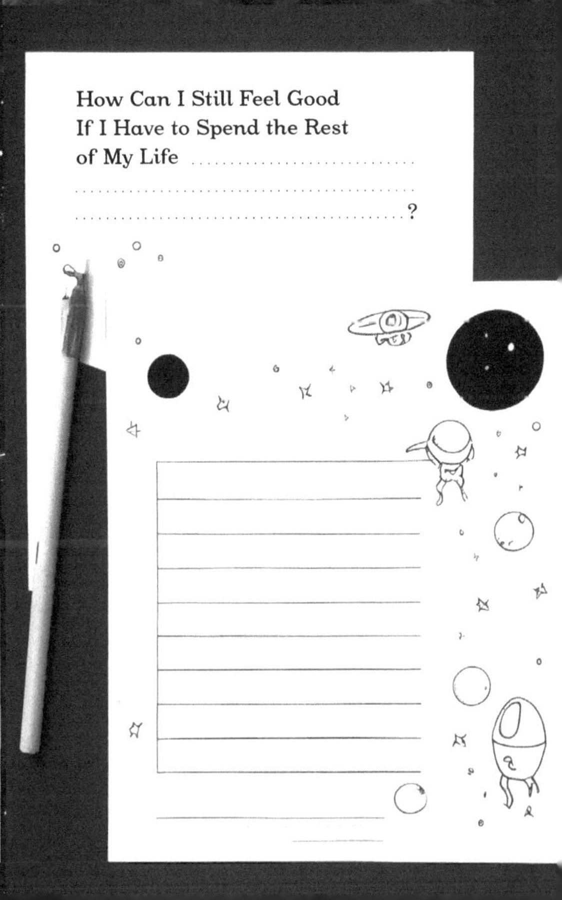
How Can I Still Feel Good
If I Have to Spend the Rest
of My Life ?

How Can I Still Feel Good If I Have to Spend the Rest of My Life ....?

How Can I Still Feel Good If I Have to Spend the Rest of My Life ....?

How Can I Still Feel Good If I Have to Spend the Rest of My Life ....?

How Can I Still Feel Good If I Have to Spend the Rest of My Life ....?

How Can I Still Feel Good
If I Have to Spend the Rest
of My Life ....
....?

How Can I Still Feel Good
If I Have to Spend the Rest
of My Life ....
....?

How Can I Still Feel Good
If I Have to Spend the Rest
of My Life ....
....?

How Can I Still Feel Good
If I Have to Spend the Rest
of My Life ....
....?

I want to stop worrying

"Alertness is the only effort. You have to be alert, not thinking in terms of change; remaining whatsoever you are good, bad, or whatsoever. One year, with no attitude of change, just being alert, suddenly one day you will find you are no more the same. Alertness will have changed everything."

—OSHO, *Book of Secrets*

Deeply Accept for a Year

Don't try to change anything! Your suffering comes from your desire to change something. When you deeply accept everything that is, you're already free.

What is a situation that you care deeply about the outcome or resolution? Write it in the third eye of one of the portraits and imagine this is a contract between you and you. You won't try to change that situation, or even think of it with an attitude of change for one year. You signed a contract! You can't try to change it! Notice how free you already feel.

"Your trying to stop it gives it strength, because by trying to stop it, you perceive it really as an enemy, and then it feeds on friction. So, let it play."

—Mooji

Let It Play

Imagine under each big top is playing one of your life's daily dramas—a situation that you want to control, change or stop. Instead of getting involved, just relax and be entertained. What experience can you decide to let play without interfering? Write the title under one of the tents and picture it as a circus act that's fun to watch. Let it play and go from being scared something will happen, to watching with curious detachment. In doing so, you will reveal how everything unfolds perfectly without your influence.

TITLE ....

TITLE ....

TITLE ....

TITLE ....

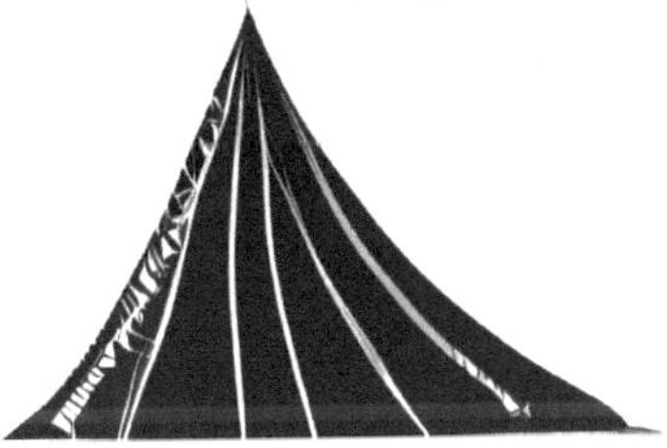

TITLE ....

TITLE ....

TITLE ....

TITLE ....

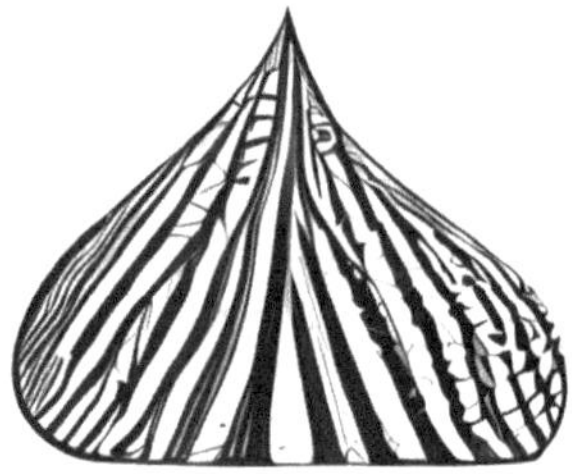

TITLE ....

TITLE ....

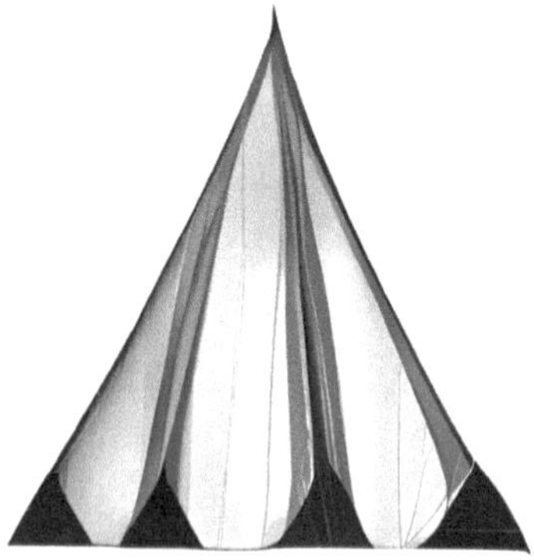

TITLE ....

TITLE ....

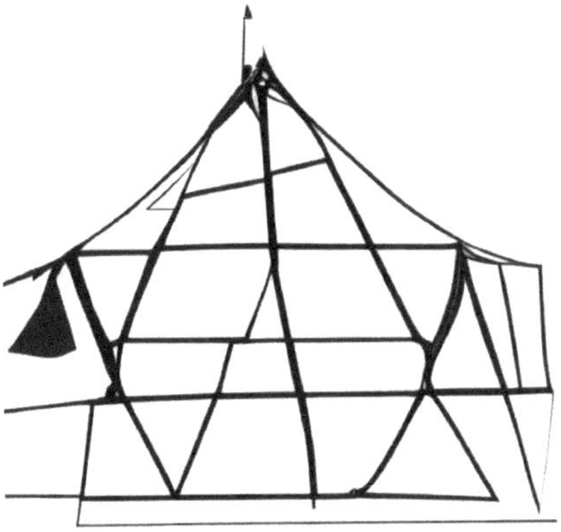

TITLE ....

TITLE ....

TITLE ....

TITLE ....

TITLE ....

TITLE ....

TITLE ....

TITLE ....

TITLE ....

TITLE ....

TITLE ....

TITLE ....

TITLE ....

TITLE ....

TITLE ....

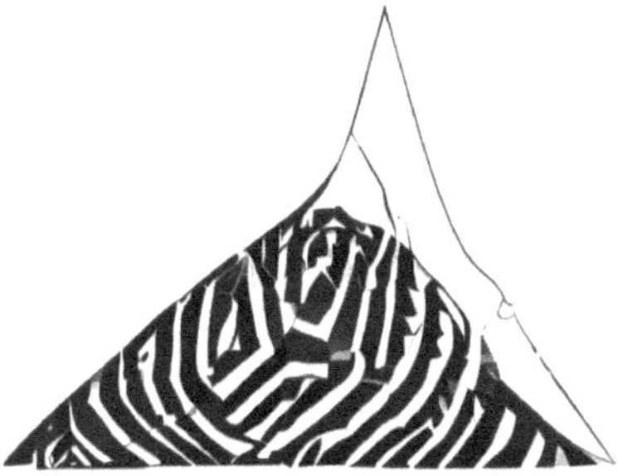

TITLE ....

TITLE ....

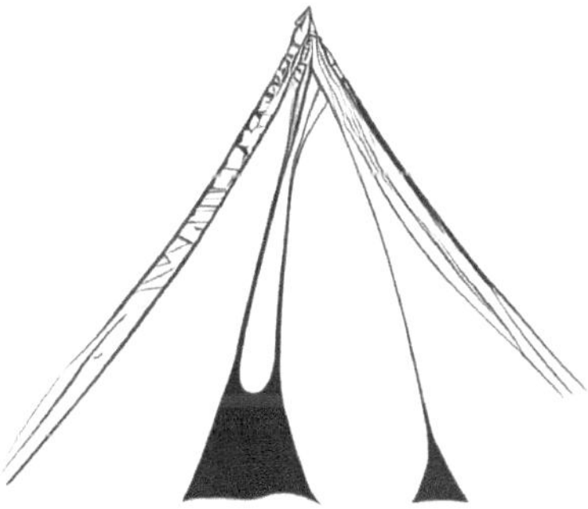

TITLE ....

How Can I Be Happy If I Never Again ______?

You know you've let something become your drug if you're afraid of losing it. What person, situation or object has become the substance you're addicted to? Write it in the label on the bottle. If you're worried about losing it, you've allowed it to eclipse your awareness of the presence of god.

How can you feel good if you never again experience the sweetness of that thing you think you need to feel good? Write it in the label and start imbibing immediately! Get addicted to the source of infinite satisfaction that is always readily available to you, and you'll never need anything else to supply it.

How Can I Be Happy If I Never Again

........................?

How Can I Be Happy If I Never Again

........................?

How Can I Be Happy If I Never Again

........................?

How Can I Be Happy If I Never Again

........................?

How Can I Be Happy If I Never Again

........................?

How Can I Be Happy If I Never Again

........................?

How Can I Be Happy If I Never Again

........................?

How Can I Be Happy If I Never Again

........................?

How Can I
Be Happy If
I Never Again

.......................?

How Can I
Be Happy If
I Never Again

.......................?

How Can I
Be Happy If
I Never Again

.......................?

How Can I
Be Happy If
I Never Again

.......................?

How Can I
Be Happy If
I Never Again

.......................?

How Can I
Be Happy If
I Never Again

.......................?

How Can I
Be Happy If
I Never Again

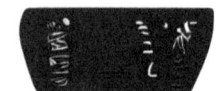

.......................?

How Can I
Be Happy If
I Never Again

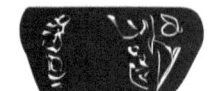

.......................?

How Can I
Be Happy If
I Never Again

......................?

How Can I
Be Happy If
I Never Again

......................?

How Can I
Be Happy If
I Never Again

......................?

How Can I
Be Happy If
I Never Again

......................?

How Can I
Be Happy If
I Never Again

......................?

How Can I
Be Happy If
I Never Again

......................?

How Can I
Be Happy If
I Never Again

......................?

How Can I
Be Happy If
I Never Again

......................?

How Can I Be Happy If I Never Again

........................?

How Can I Be Happy If I Never Again

........................?

How Can I Be Happy If I Never Again

........................?

How Can I Be Happy If I Never Again

........................?

How Can I Be Happy If I Never Again

........................?

How Can I Be Happy If I Never Again

........................?

How Can I Be Happy If I Never Again

........................?

How Can I Be Happy If I Never Again

........................?

How Can I
Be Happy If
I Never Again

……………………?

How Can I
Be Happy If
I Never Again

……………………?

How Can I
Be Happy If
I Never Again

……………………?

How Can I
Be Happy If
I Never Again

……………………?

How Can I
Be Happy If
I Never Again

……………………?

How Can I
Be Happy If
I Never Again

……………………?

How Can I
Be Happy If
I Never Again

……………………?

How Can I
Be Happy If
I Never Again

……………………?

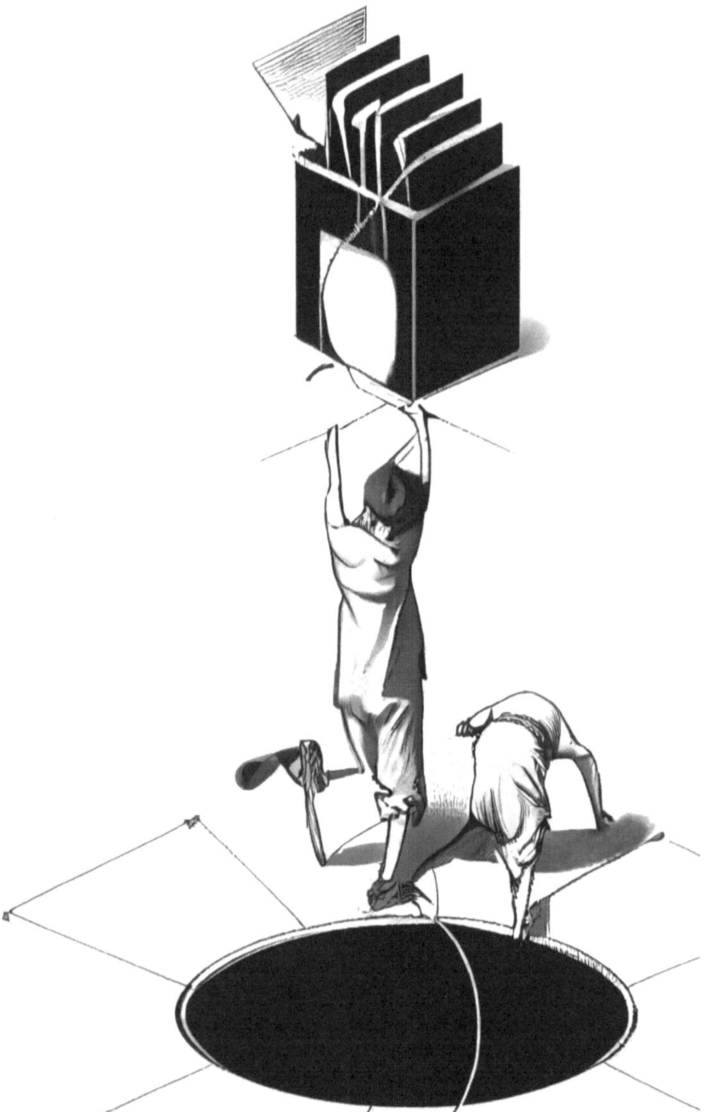

I want help

Spell for Connection

If we don't stop to examine what we want and why we think it will make us happy, we will chase desires over and over and wonder why it's never enough. Let your intuition tell you the real source of happiness by investigating the roots of your desires.

Why do you think it will make you happy? We spend so much time in our heads thinking about the thing we need to happen in order to be happy, but do we ever stop to ask ourselves *why* that situation will make us happy? It usually comes down to feeling loved and secure. But as you know, nothing outside of you is your true supply of love or security.

Write down what you think will make you happy and why. Then ask the *all-knowing wizard within* what the source of what you seek is. What do you hear?

What do I think will
make me happy?

Why do I think it will
make me happy?

My intuition tells me the
source of the above is:

What do I think will make me happy?

Why do I think it will make me happy?

My intuition tells me the source of the above is:

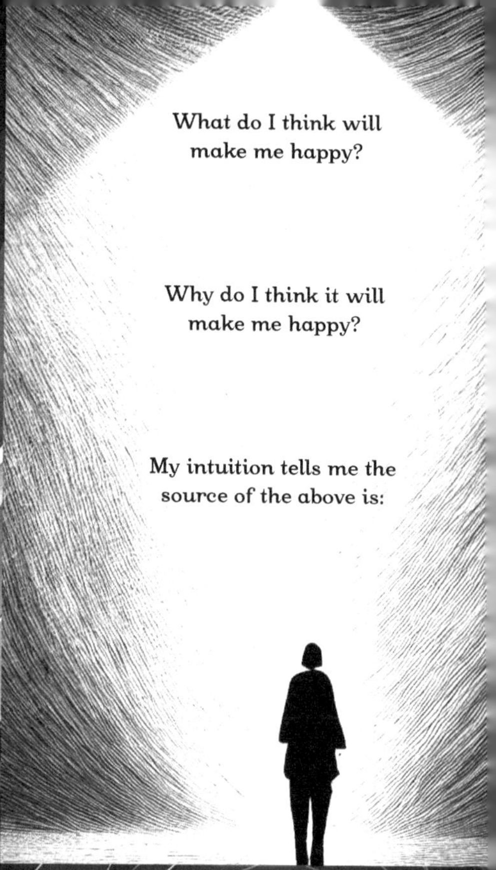

What do I think will make me happy?

Why do I think it will make me happy?

My intuition tells me the source of the above is:

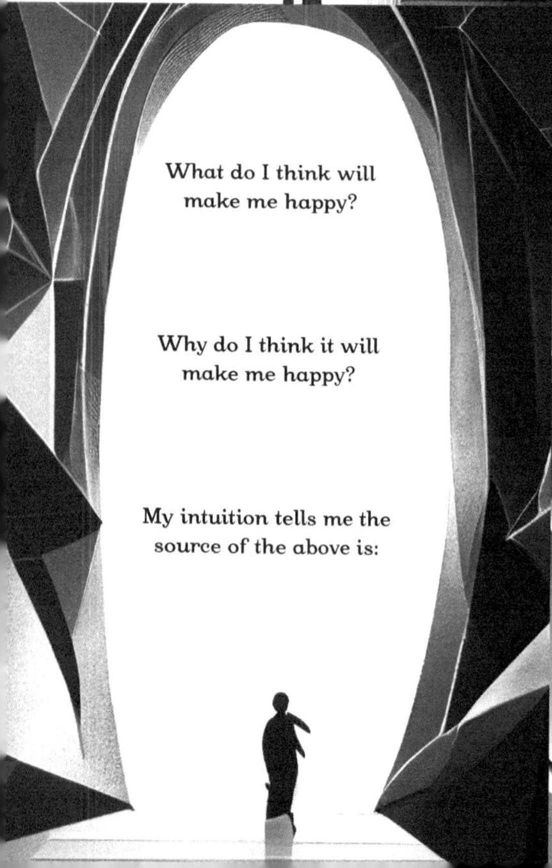

What do I think will make me happy?

Why do I think it will make me happy?

My intuition tells me the source of the above is:

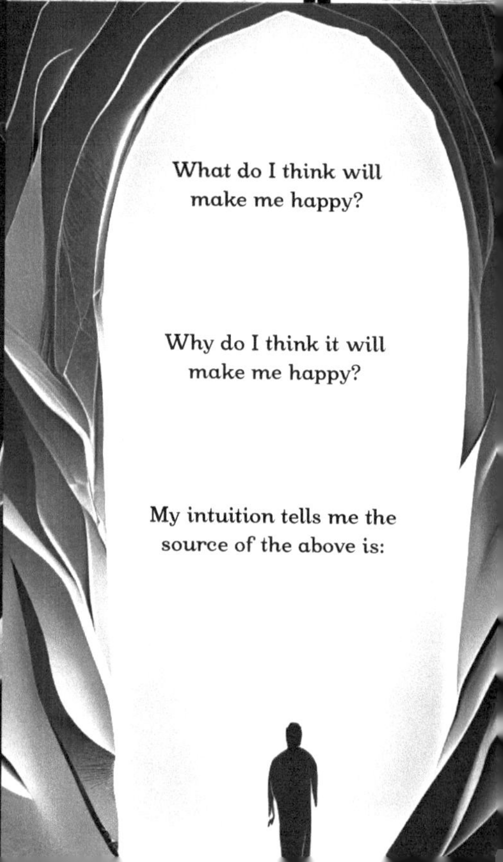

What do I think will make me happy?

Why do I think it will make me happy?

My intuition tells me the source of the above is:

What do I think will make me happy?
Why do I think it will make me happy?
My intuition tells me the source of the above is:

What do I think will make me happy?
Why do I think it will make me happy?
My intuition tells me the source of the above is:

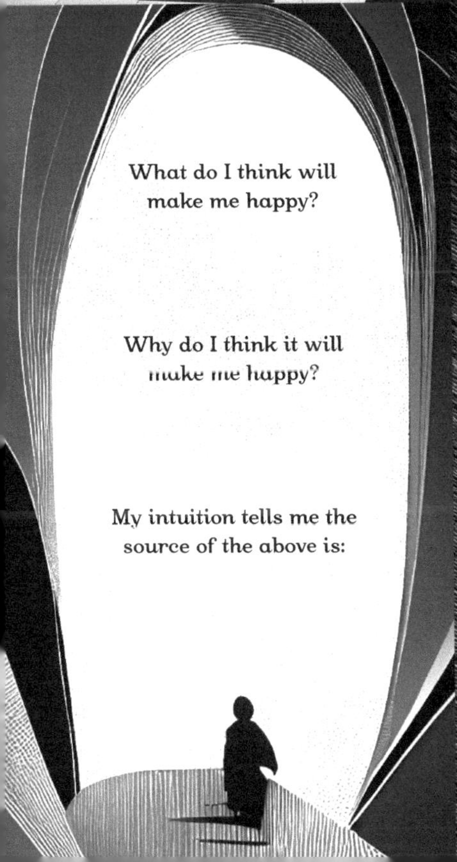
What do I think will make me happy?
Why do I think it will make me happy?
My intuition tells me the source of the above is:

What do I think will make me happy?
Why do I think it will make me happy?
My intuition tells me the source of the above is:

What do I think will make me happy?
Why do I think it will make me happy?
My intuition tells me the source of the above is:

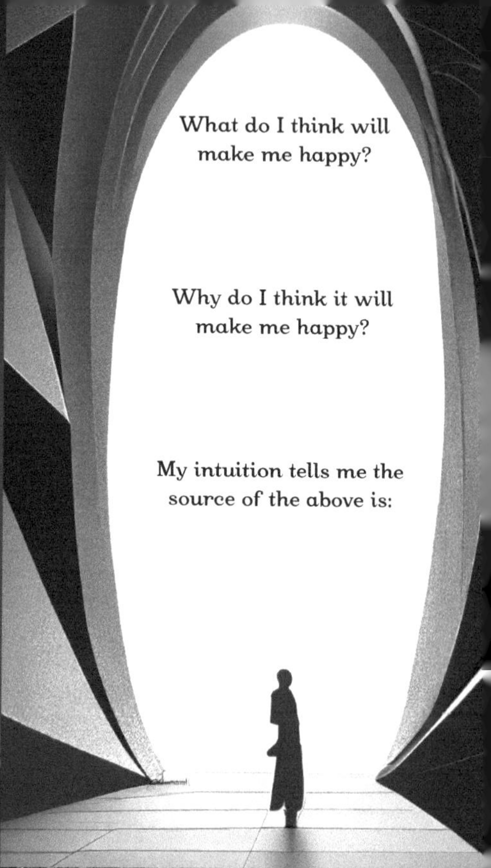
What do I think will make me happy?
Why do I think it will make me happy?
My intuition tells me the source of the above is:

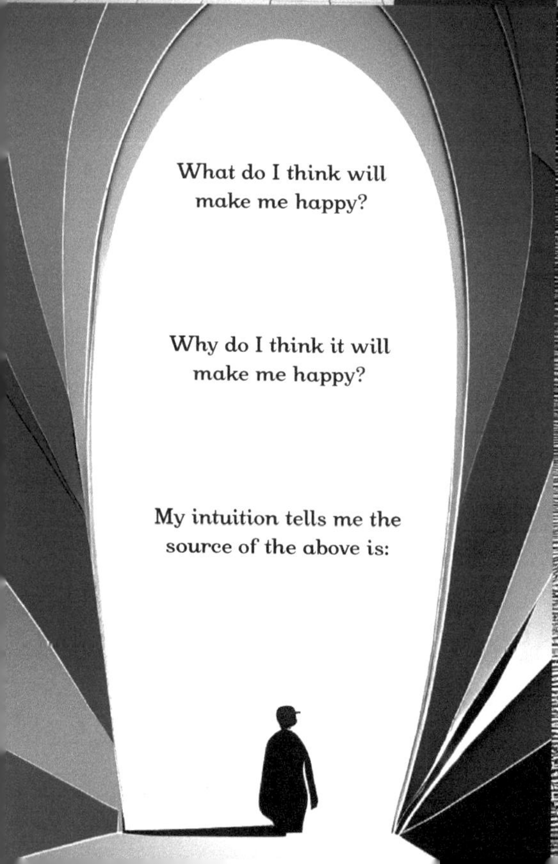
What do I think will make me happy?
Why do I think it will make me happy?
My intuition tells me the source of the above is:

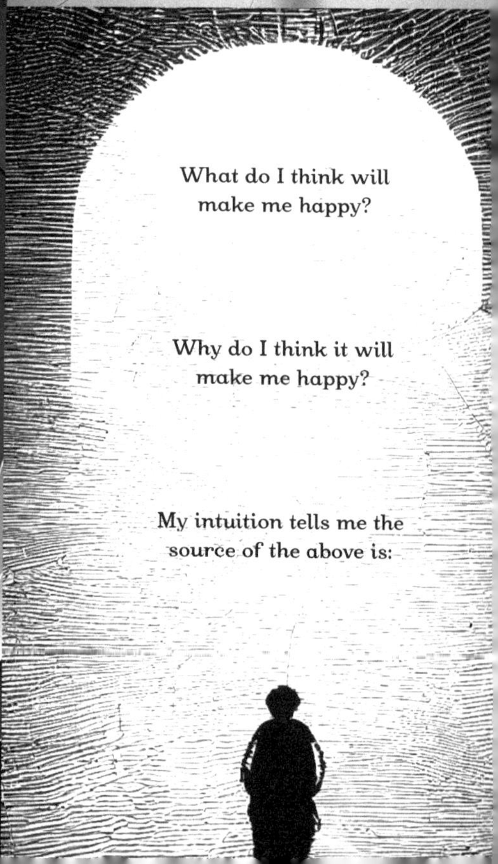
What do I think will make me happy?
Why do I think it will make me happy?
My intuition tells me the source of the above is:

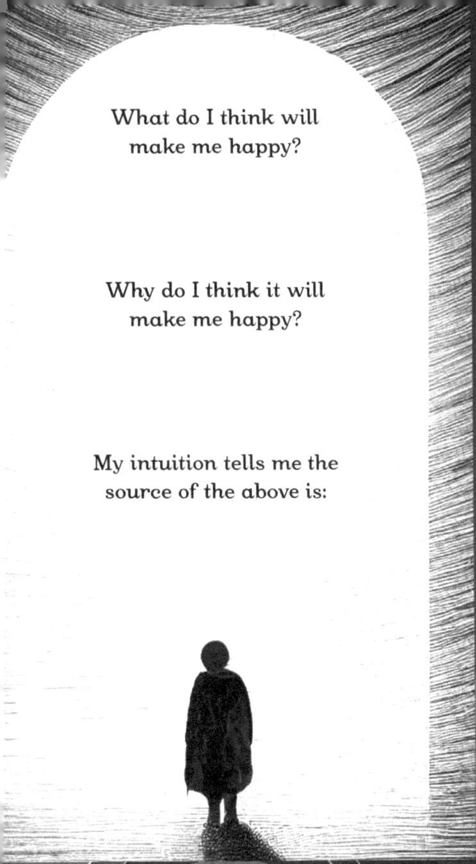
What do I think will make me happy?
Why do I think it will make me happy?
My intuition tells me the source of the above is:

What do I think will make me happy?
Why do I think it will make me happy?
My intuition tells me the source of the above is:

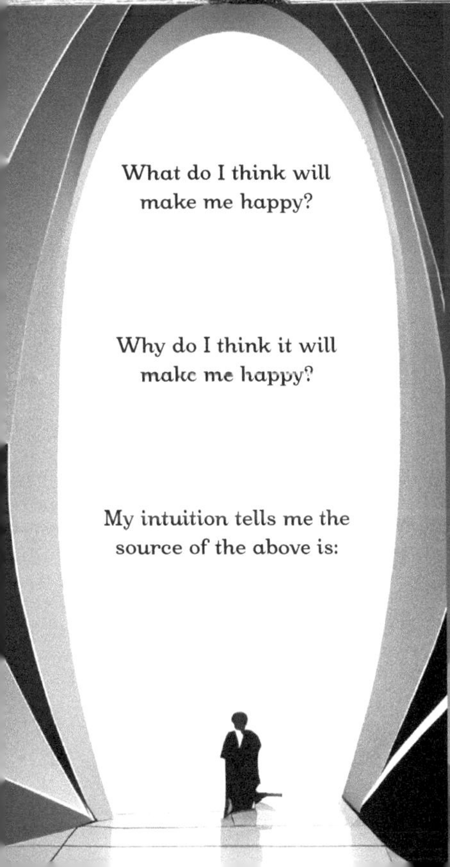
What do I think will make me happy?
Why do I think it will make me happy?
My intuition tells me the source of the above is:

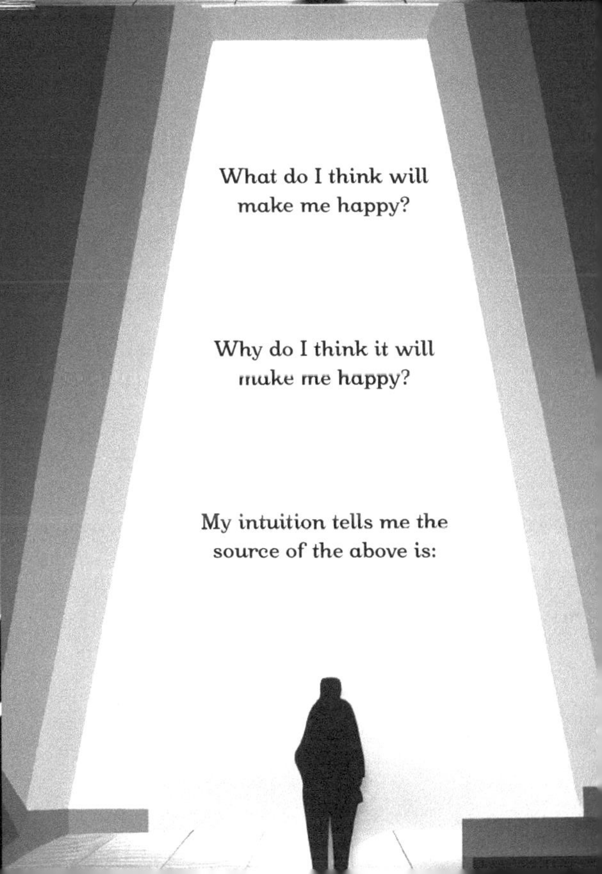
What do I think will make me happy?
Why do I think it will make me happy?
My intuition tells me the source of the above is:

"Relaxing and letting go of struggle isn't something that the ego does—yet we often get our egos involved in trying to make letting go happen. To even say, "Let go of struggle," isn't quite right. All that's required is that you begin to notice that place within you that's not struggling. To do this means there's really no future for which to hope. In fact, the idea of the future is one of the barriers of awakening to our true nature. This is because the future keeps us looking at something other than what's happening right now.

If you were to ask yourself, "Even before I try to stop struggling, even before I try to relax and find peace, is peace already here?" Then just be quiet for a moment, and listen. We assume that what we're seeking isn't already present. Of course that's why we're seeking it: because we believe that peace and happiness and freedom aren't here, right where we are, right now, already. The assumption that what we're seeking, some state of completion, isn't here right now is what causes us to look for it, to start the search."

—Adyashanti, *Falling Into Grace*

Notice the Place Within You That's Not Struggling

On the surface of life you feel the attack of every storm ravaging your branches and leaves, but the majority of who you are lies deep and unaffected underneath the passing winds of change. You may be struggling with the events of your life, or rather the thoughts in your mind, but the *real you* isn't struggling at all. It's just existing. Notice that part, then describe it in one of the cards. Make noticing it your only pursuit and you'll realize it's who you really are.

"I will leave everything to the supreme so that my own actions, thoughts, feelings and my response to them automatically are like the lord's responses to them."

—Mooji

Thank You God for Replacing Me with You

Mooji suggests praying "Thank you god for replacing me with you" when you're suffering your preferences and want to surrender but are having a hard time letting go of control. Whenever you get stressed about wanting things to be a certain way, ask god to replace you. Then you will know for sure all of your actions are divine. You are no longer the separate you. You're the complete you, not the manipulative, ego-identified you. What is a situation you are struggling to make go your way? In a blank oval on a card, write down how god feels about the matter and become totally confident in letting go and letting god lead the way.

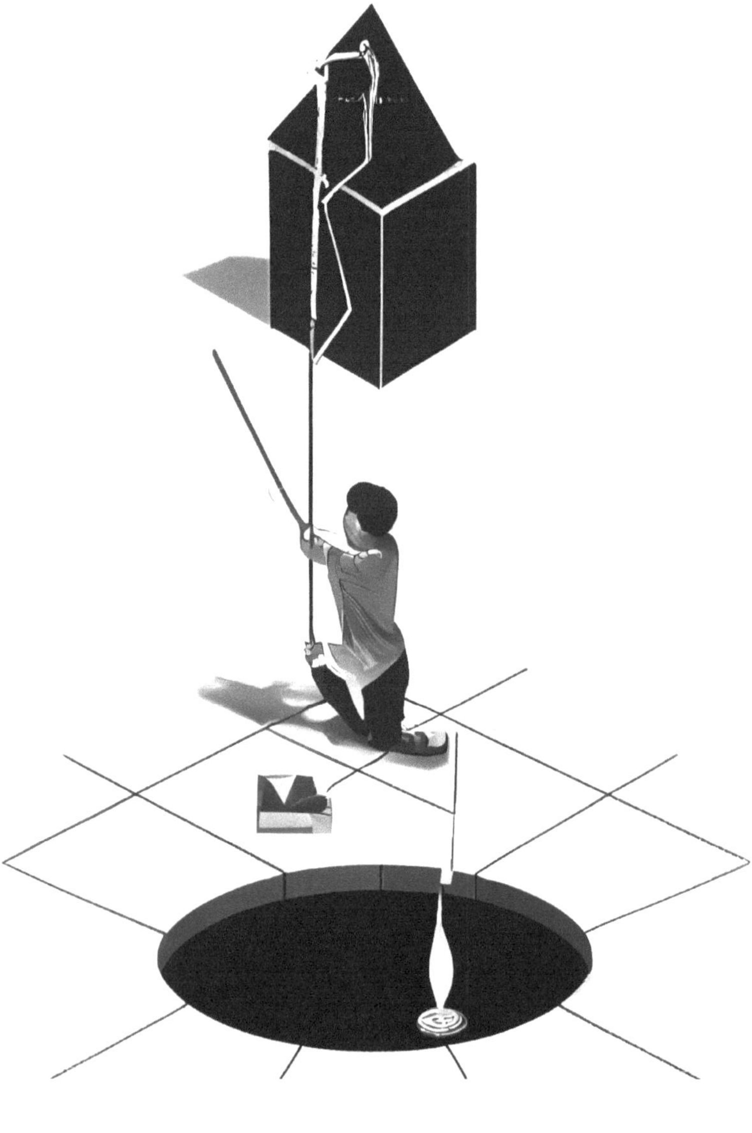

I want something specific

Spell for Manifesting

The mirror can reflect wanting or the mirror can reflect having, which do you prefer? When you want something, you're constantly recreating a situation of wanting it. Choose it, and it's already yours. If consciousness is the only reality, physical experience can only show you your inner world. Choose it first and by the feeling of having it, it will appear.

What do I want?

How does it feel
to want, not have?

What do I choose?

How does it feel
to choose, not want?

What do I want?
How does it feel
to want, not have?
What do I choose?
How does it feel
to choose, not want?
What do I want?
How does it feel
to want, not have?
What do I choose?
How does it feel
to choose, not want?
What do I want?
How does it feel
to want, not have?
What do I choose?
How does it feel
to choose, not want?
What do I want?
How does it feel
to want, not have?
What do I choose?
How does it feel
to choose, not want?

What do I want?
How does it feel to want, not have?
What do I choose?
How does it feel to choose, not want?
What do I want?
How does it feel to want, not have?
What do I choose?
How does it feel to choose, not want?
What do I want?
How does it feel to want, not have?
What do I choose?
How does it feel to choose, not want?
What do I want?
How does it feel to want, not have?
What do I choose?
How does it feel to choose, not want?

What do I want?

How does it feel
to want, not have?

What do I choose?

How does it feel
to choose, not want?

What do I want?

How does it feel
to want, not have?

What do I choose?

How does it feel
to choose, not want?

What do I want?

How does it feel
to want, not have?

What do I choose?

How does it feel
to choose, not want?

What do I want?

How does it feel
to want, not have?

What do I choose?

How does it feel
to choose, not want?

What do I want?
How does it feel to want, not have?
What do I choose?
How does it feel to choose, not want?
What do I want?
How does it feel to want, not have?
What do I choose?
How does it feel to choose, not want?
What do I want?
How does it feel to want, not have?
What do I choose?
How does it feel to choose, not want?
What do I want?
How does it feel to want, not have?
What do I choose?
How does it feel to choose, not want?

The Annunciation

Neville Goddard taught that feeling precedes all physical experience. If one can feel the feeling of their desire fulfilled, then by universal law, that feeling must manifest. One of Neville's most effective methods for feeling the feeling of your desire fulfilled is to imagine yourself telling a good friend about your success, then imagine their reaction to your success.

Your subconscious doesn't know the difference between reality and imagination, and when you live that experience in your imagination, your subconscious accepts it as true. What your subconscious believes to be true, will appear in your conscious reality. Imagine telling your friend your success by writing it on the **Statement** card. Then imagine what your friend will say to congratulate you and write it in the **Reply** card.

Statement
Reply

Statement
Reply

Statement
Reply

Statement
Reply

Statement
Reply

Statement
Reply

Statement
Reply

Statement
Reply

Statement
Reply

Statement
Reply

Statement
Reply

Statement
Reply

Statement
Reply

Statement
Reply

Statement
Reply

Statement
Reply

Statement
Reply

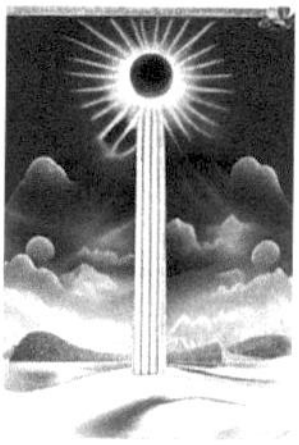

"There is nothing noble in wanting what is not. There is nothing noble in depreciating the mystery of this moment as it is and wanting something different instead.

—Kat Adamson

Unhappy Either Way

When you prefer one outcome over another, and you tell yourself, "I'll be happy either way," the mind immediately rejects that notion because it is already biased toward its clear preference. But when you tell yourself you'll be unhappy either way, the mind immediately agrees. The mind loves misery! The mind is misery!

An important recognition also happens. You realize you will be unhappy either way because the mind is always looking for problems. If you have a preference, you'll be unhappy. When you realize you'll be unhappy either way, you stop preferring, and then through the act of stopping the mind, you're happy either way.

Write down what you want and what you don't want in the columns provided. Then write down the potential problems that may accompany each outcome. Now that you see there will be more problems either way, why bother preferring? Absolutely no problems will arise from you deciding not to care about the outcome!

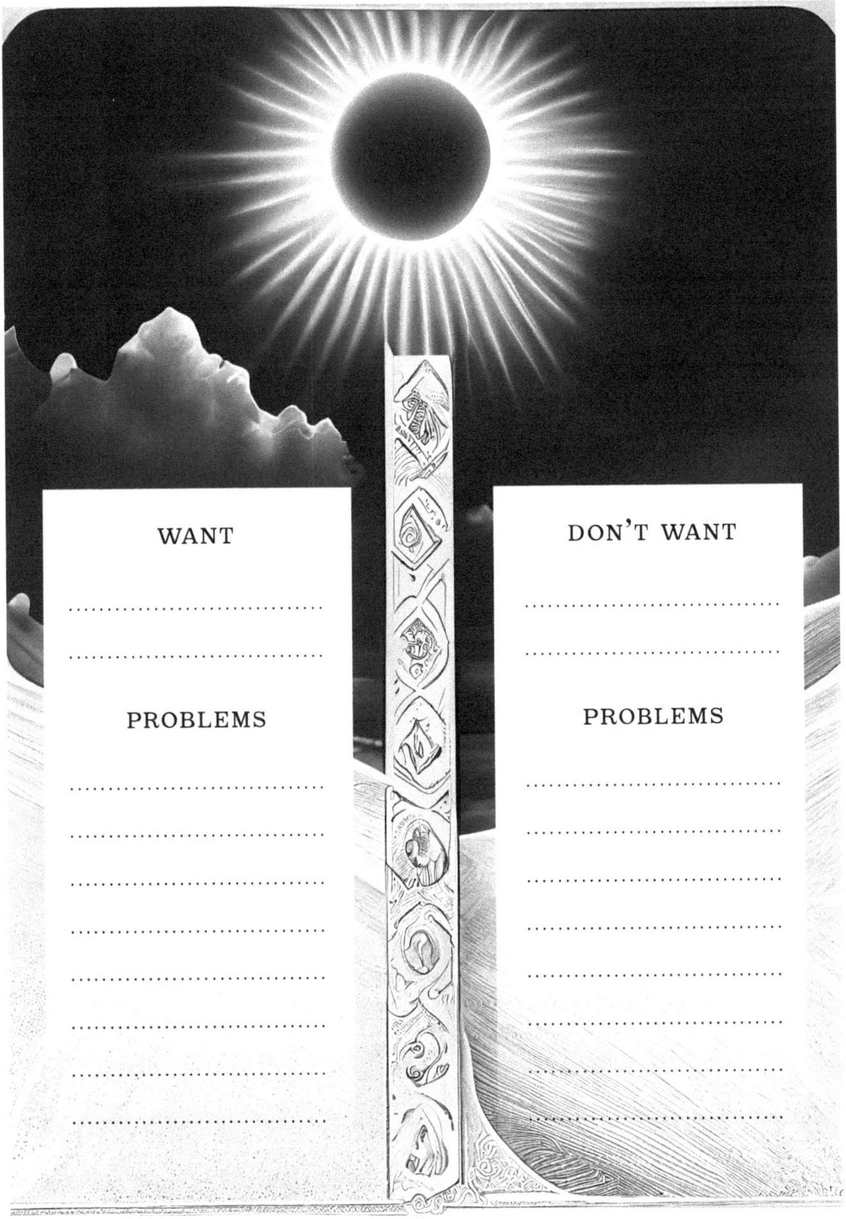
WANT
PROBLEMS
DON'T WANT
PROBLEMS

WANT
PROBLEMS
DON'T WANT
PROBLEMS

WANT
PROBLEMS
DON'T WANT
PROBLEMS

WANT
PROBLEMS
DON'T WANT
PROBLEMS

WANT
PROBLEMS
DON'T WANT
PROBLEMS

WANT
PROBLEMS
DON'T WANT
PROBLEMS

WANT
PROBLEMS
DON'T WANT
PROBLEMS

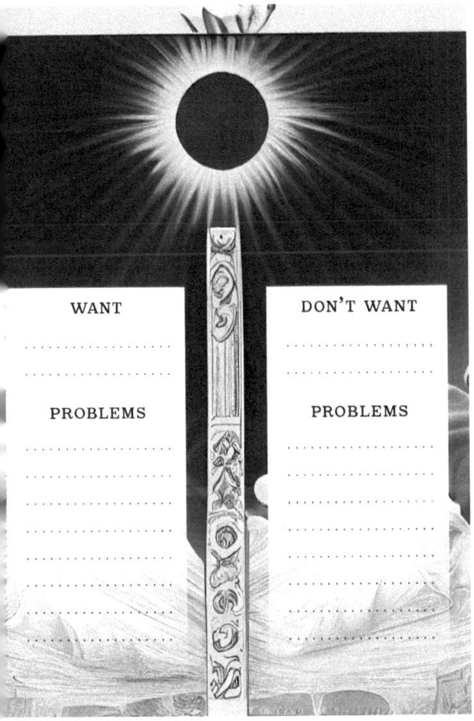
WANT
PROBLEMS
DON'T WANT
PROBLEMS

WANT
PROBLEMS
DON'T WANT
PROBLEMS

WANT
PROBLEMS
DON'T WANT
PROBLEMS

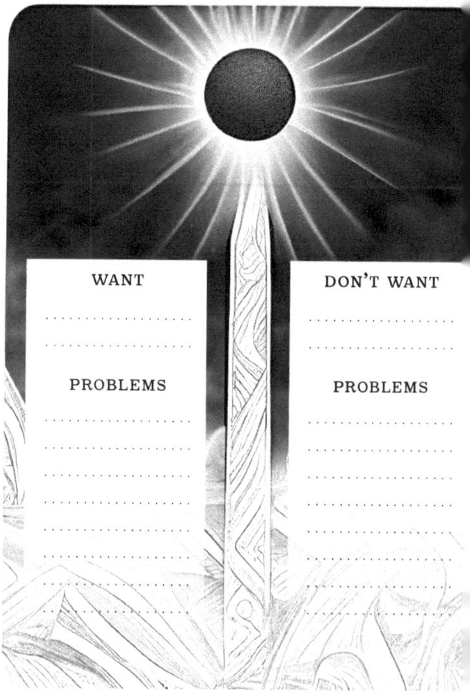
WANT
PROBLEMS
DON'T WANT
PROBLEMS

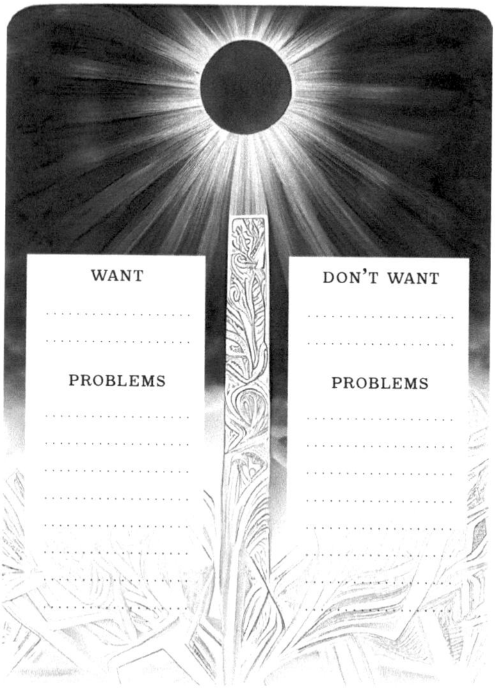
WANT
PROBLEMS
DON'T WANT
PROBLEMS

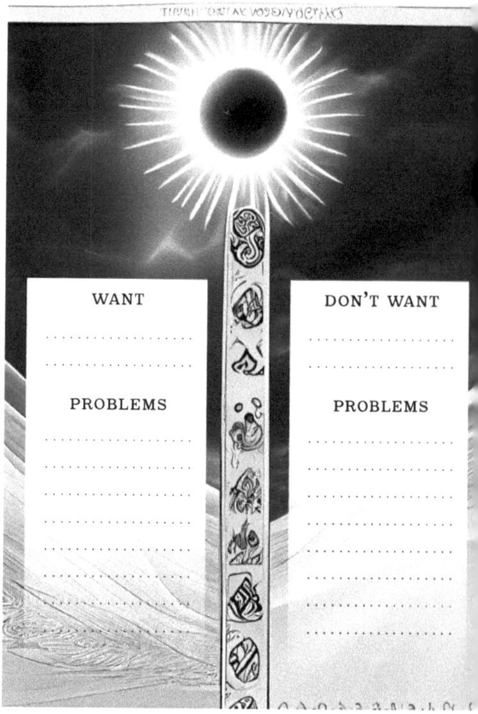
WANT
PROBLEMS
DON'T WANT
PROBLEMS

WANT
DON'T WANT
PROBLEMS
PROBLEMS

WANT
DON'T WANT
PROBLEMS
PROBLEMS

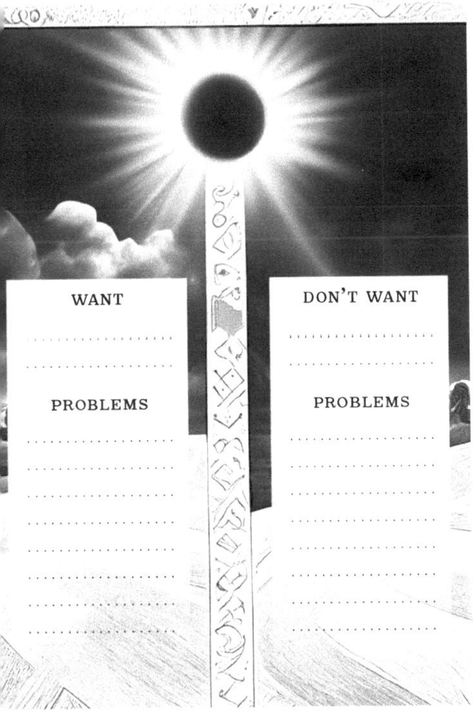
WANT
DON'T WANT
PROBLEMS
PROBLEMS

WANT
DON'T WANT
PROBLEMS
PROBLEMS

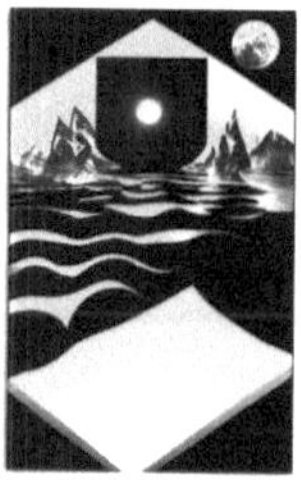

"If you would say: 'I remember when I couldn't afford to spend $400 a month for rent,' you are implying you can well afford it now. The words: 'I remember when it was a struggle to live on my monthly income,' implies you have transcended that limitation. You can put yourself into any state by remembering when."

—Neville Goddard

Remember When?

If you're constantly thinking to yourself, "I can't wait until I can afford my rent with no problems," or, "My ship will come in soon," or "I hope I can make ends meet," you're expressing through your consciousness that you don't yet have those things. Life responds accordingly and depicts a reality without those things–a reality in which you're perpetually suspended in hope and anticipation. In order to see it, you must tell life you already have it. You must assume the feeling place of already having your desires fulfilled.

Be the person that already has it now, and firmly state to yourself, "I remember when I hadn't yet ________," and write it in the life raft. Now you know you're already saved. You can relax in how far you have come!

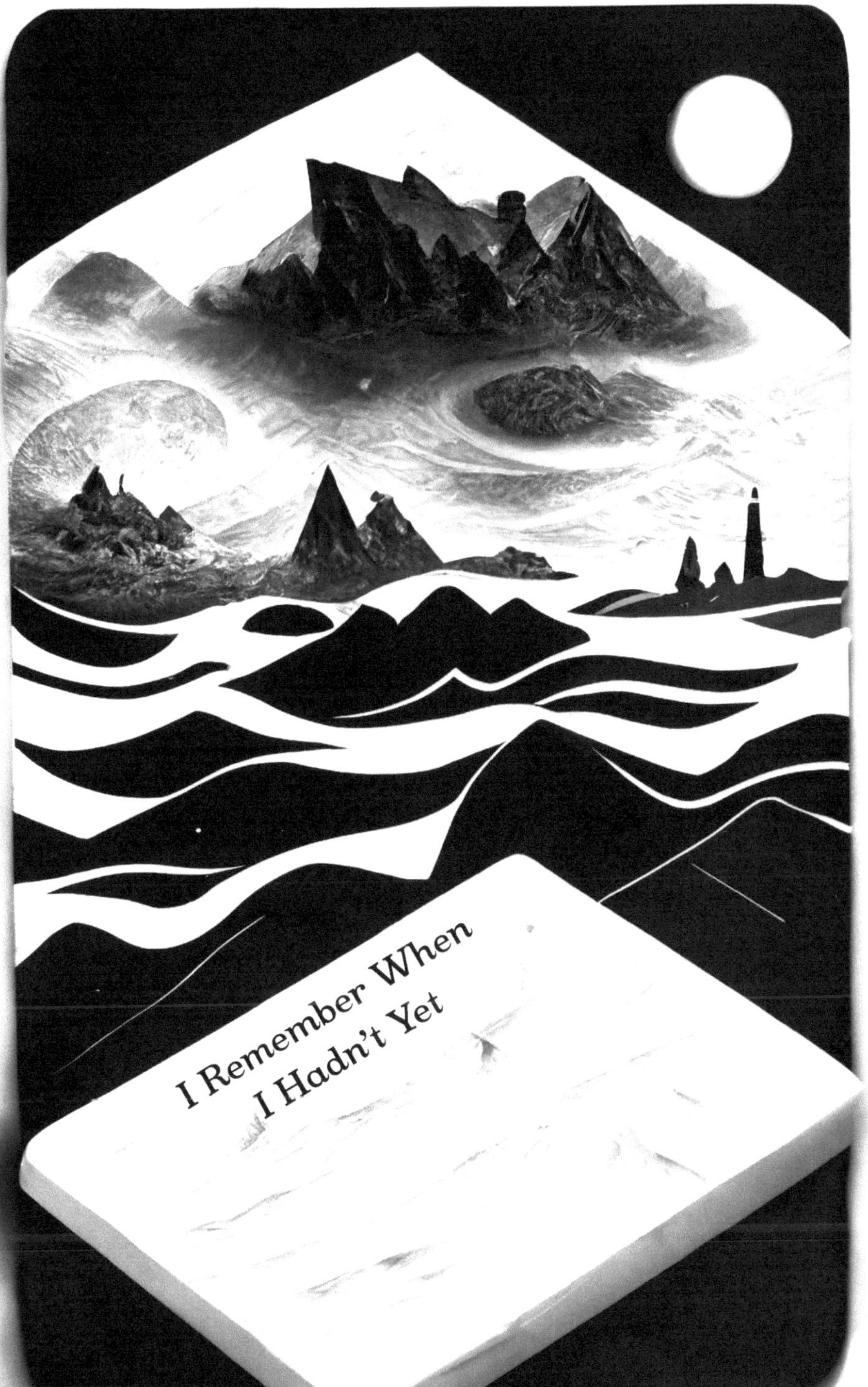
I Remember When
I Hadn't Yet

I Remember When
I Hadn't Yet

I Remember When
I Hadn't Yet
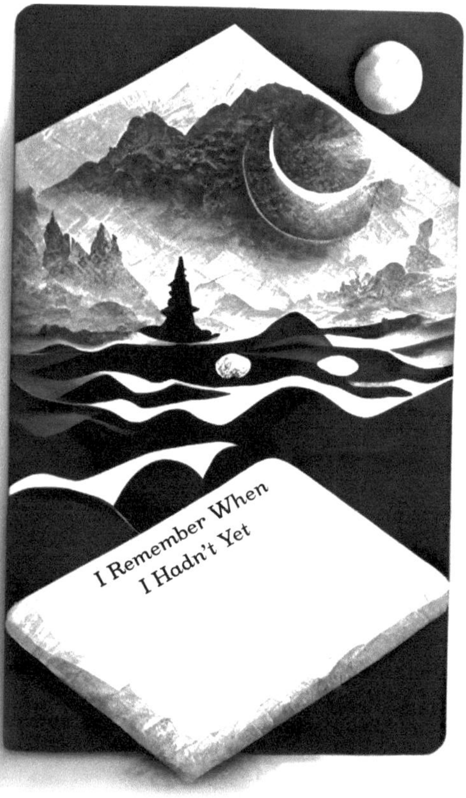
I Remember When
I Hadn't Yet

I Remember When
I Hadn't Yet

I Remember When
I Hadn't Yet

I Remember When
I Hadn't Yet

I Remember When
I Hadn't Yet

I Remember When
I Hadn't Yet

I Remember When
I Hadn't Yet

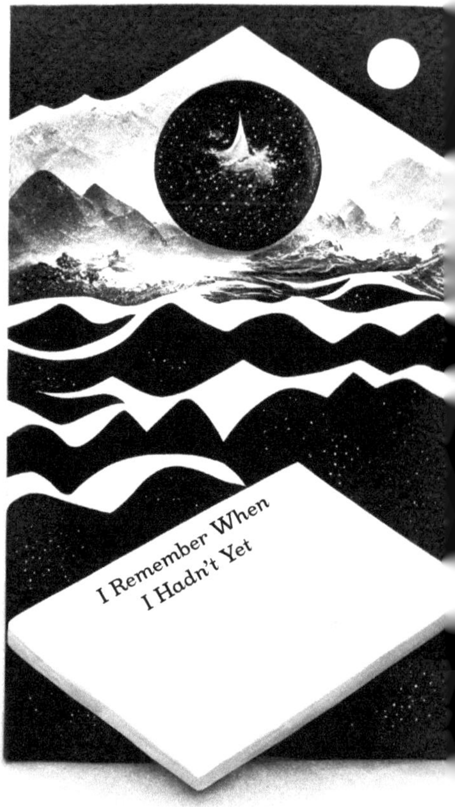
I Remember When
I Hadn't Yet

I Remember When
I Hadn't Yet

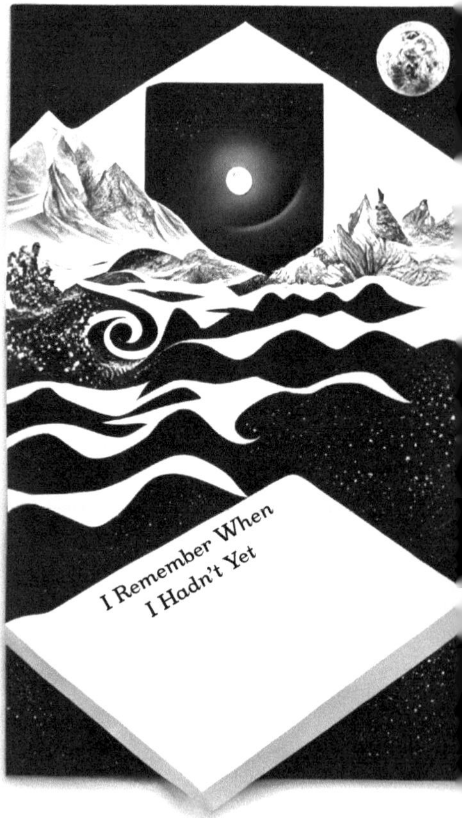
I Remember When
I Hadn't Yet

I Remember When
I Hadn't Yet

I Remember When
I Hadn't Yet

I Remember When
I Hadn't Yet

I Remember When
I Hadn't Yet

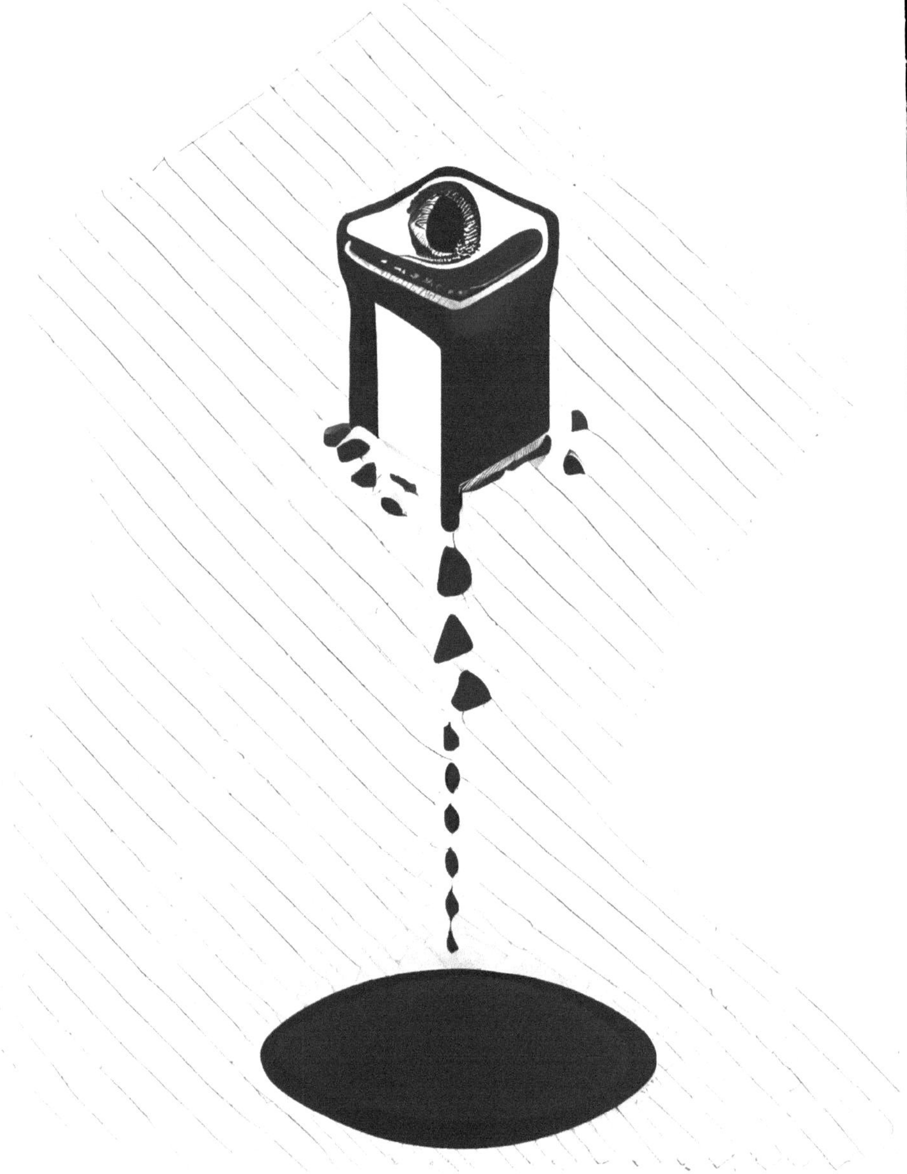

I got what I wanted but I'm still not happy

Refuse to Suffer

You got what you wanted but now you need MORE. And when you get more, more won't even be enough. It will never be enough because, even though it feels like it, the manifestation isn't the source of the satisfied feelings–you are. If you're attached to a manifestation and you can't stop seeking it, stop and ask yourself what exactly is it you're still seeking? When you ask what you are still looking for, your attention turns to look at itself. In this looking, the attention is no longer looking outward for worldly satisfaction but is instead resting peacefully on itself. Turning the seeking to look at itself drops the search and peace is revealed.

Write down the manifestation you got that you're now attached to. Now ponder what you're still seeking. You'll get some reflex answers at first, but dig deeper. What are you *really* seeking?

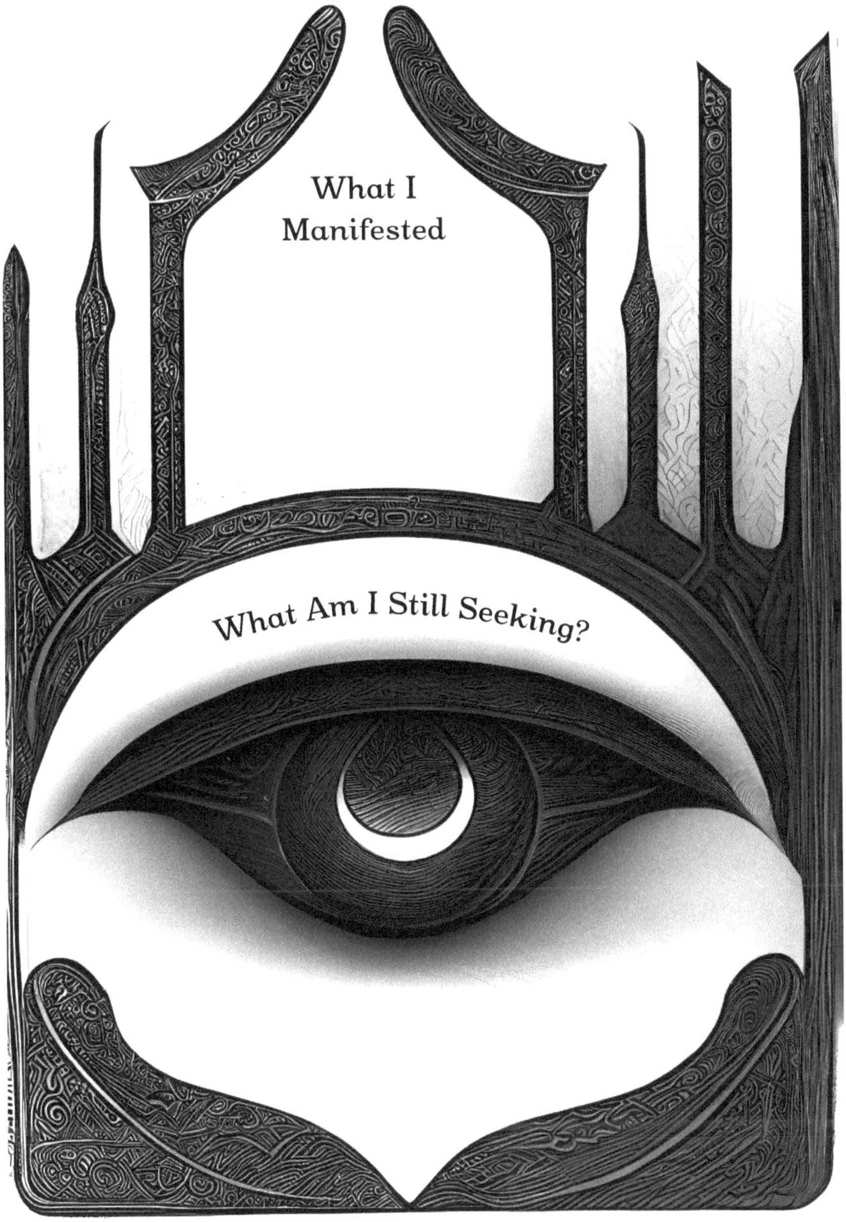
What I
Manifested
What Am I Still Seeking?

What I
Manifested
What Am I Still Seeking?

What I
Manifested
What Am I Still Seeking?

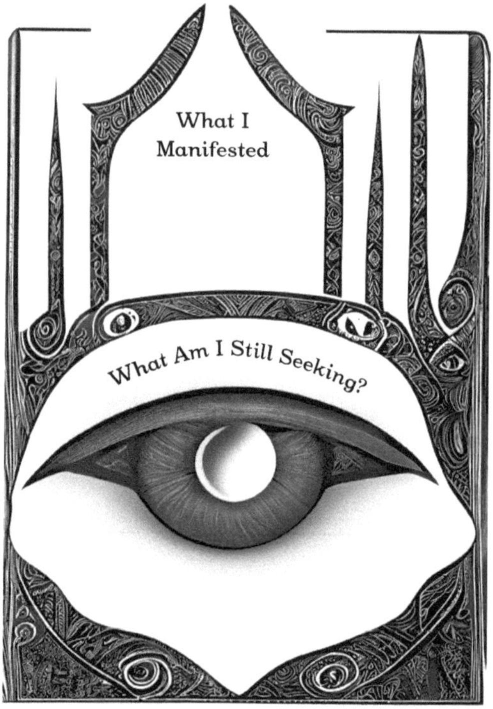
What I
Manifested
What Am I Still Seeking?

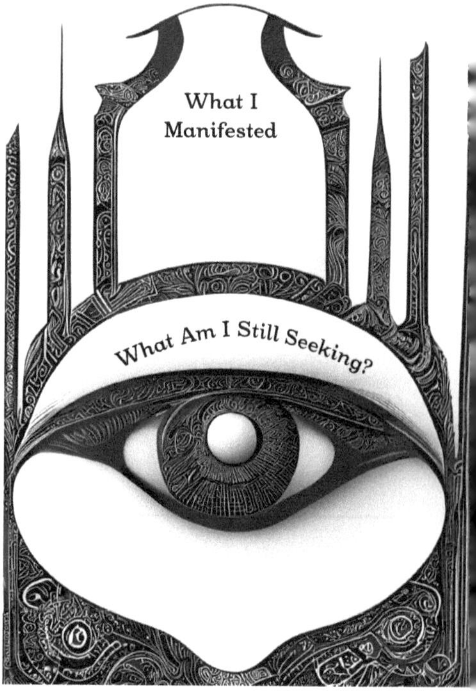
What I
Manifested
What Am I Still Seeking?

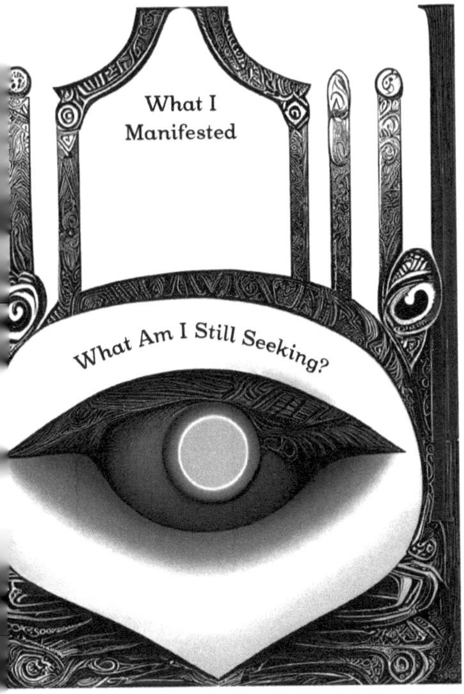
What I
Manifested
What Am I Still Seeking?

What I
Manifested
What Am I Still Seeking?

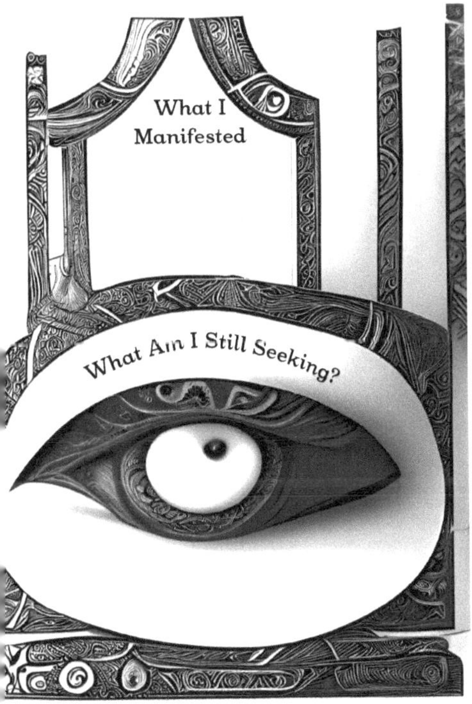
What I
Manifested
What Am I Still Seeking?

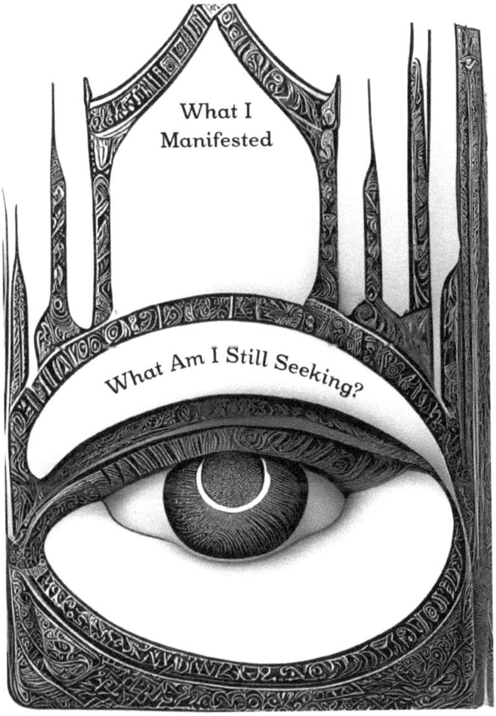
What I
Manifested
What Am I Still Seeking?

What I
Manifested
What Am I Still Seeking?

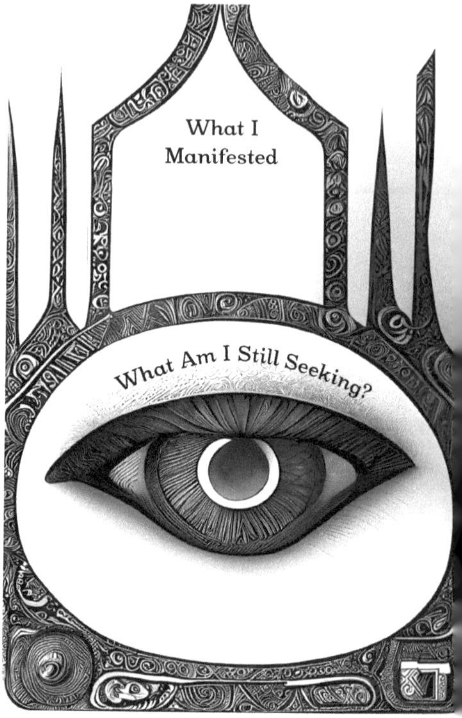
What I
Manifested
What Am I Still Seeking?

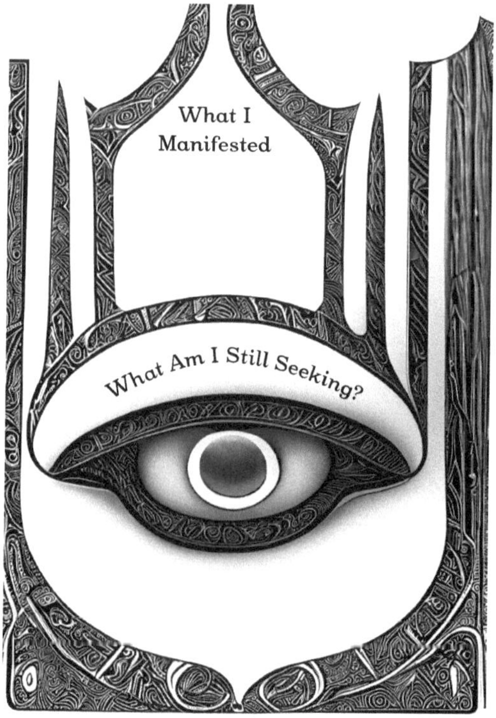
What I
Manifested
What Am I Still Seeking?

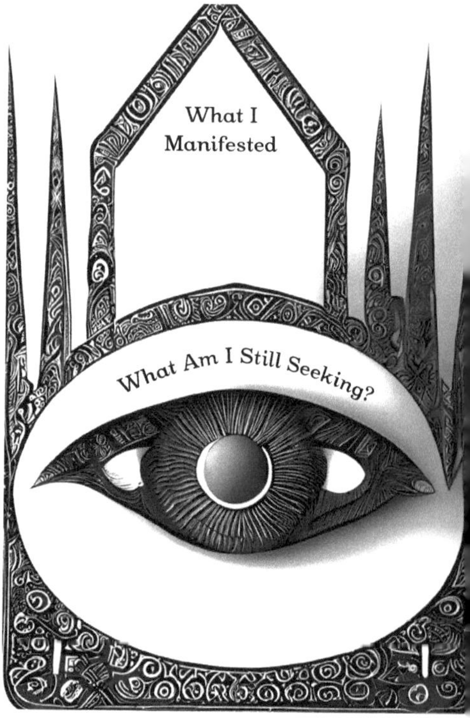
What I
Manifested
What Am I Still Seeking?

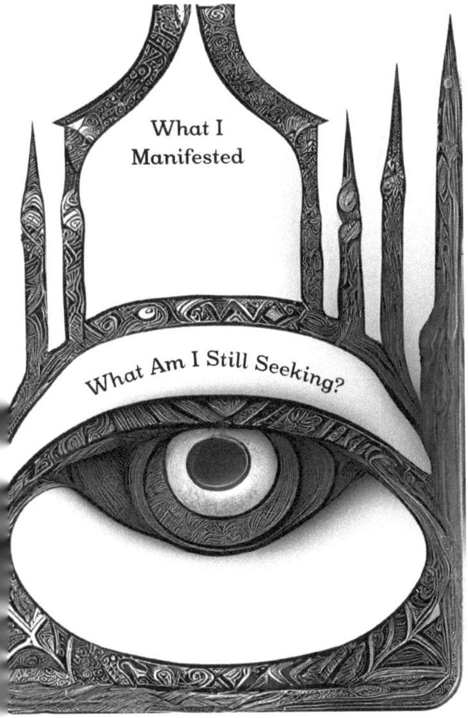
What I
Manifested
What Am I Still Seeking?

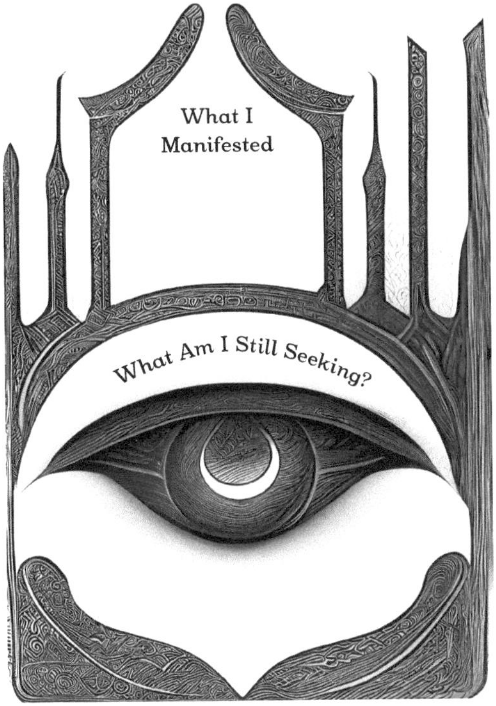
What I
Manifested
What Am I Still Seeking?

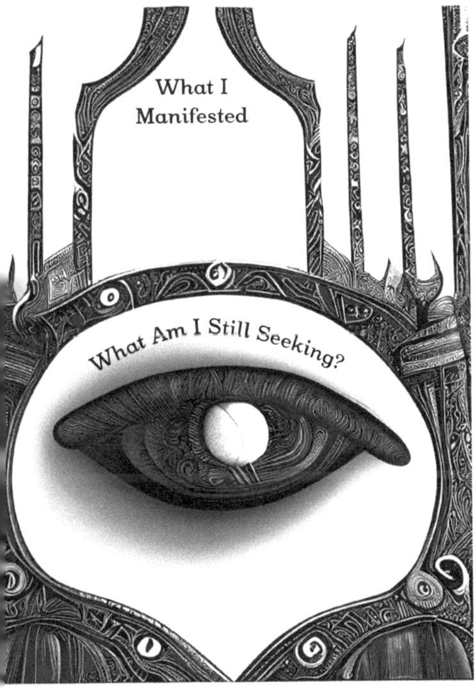
What I
Manifested
What Am I Still Seeking?

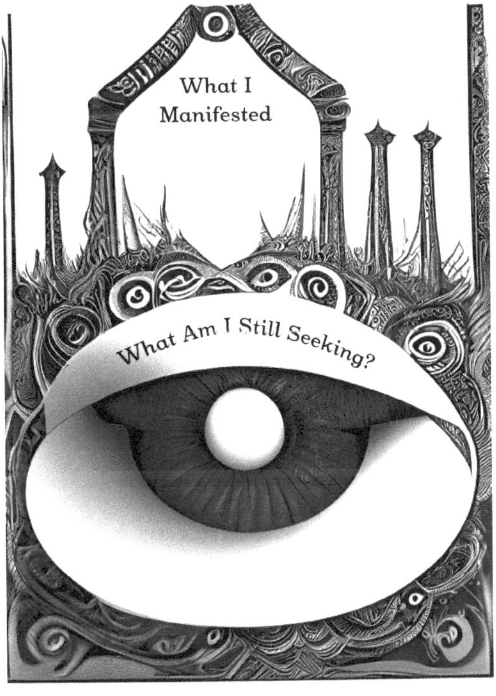
What I
Manifested
What Am I Still Seeking?

"You are awareness. Awareness is another name for you. Since you are awareness there is no need to attain or cultivate it. All that you have to do is to give up being aware of other things, that are of the not-Self. If one gives up being aware of them then pure awareness alone remains, and that is the Self."

—Sri Ramana Maharshi

What Am I Not?

By noticing everything you are not, you reveal who you really are. If you got what you wanted but still want more more more, list in the blank spaces all the things that your ego tells you you need but actually are illusions. You are not your weight, your family, your income, your job, your success, your service, your memory, your body, your ideas, your thoughts… Keep going and going until you see who you really are.

It Won't Always Be Like This

When you get what you want and you love it so so so much, it can feel so scary to imagine ever going without. But you are the powerful creator who manifested such pleasures. When you get too attached to the beauty you create, go back to the state you were in to make such creations possible.

Write down the manifestation you're attached to—that thing you're afraid of losing–in the top treasure box. Now write how you manifested it in the lower box. This is the true foundation of that feeling you seek, not the manifestation. Return to your source and you'll realize *nothing* can ever take that feeling away.

Manifestation
I'm Attached to
How I Manifested It

Manifestation
I'm Attached to
How I Manifested It

Manifestation
I'm Attached to
How I Manifested It
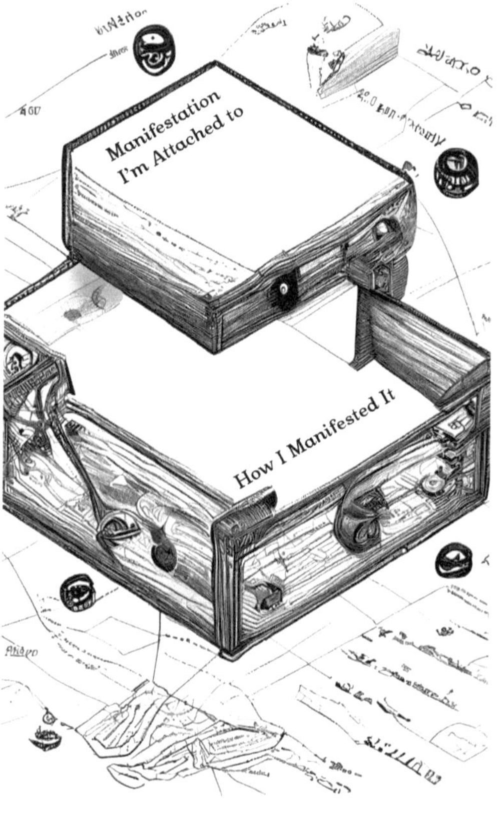
Manifestation
I'm Attached to
How I Manifested It
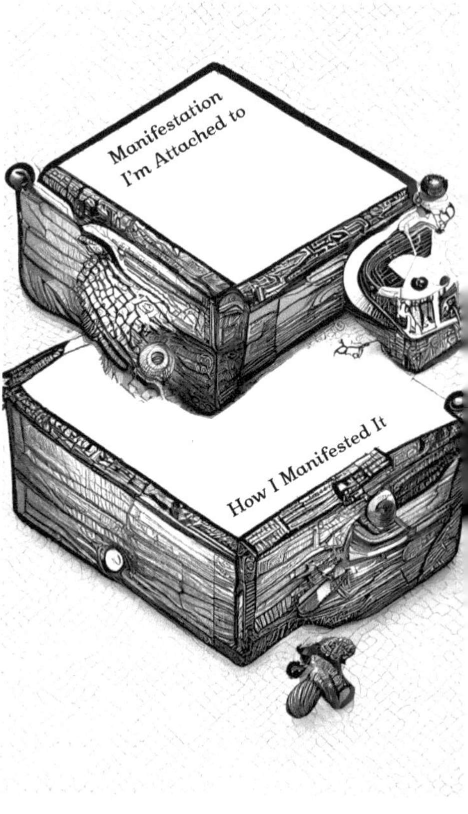
Manifestation
I'm Attached to
How I Manifested It

Manifestation
I'm Attached to
How I Manifested It

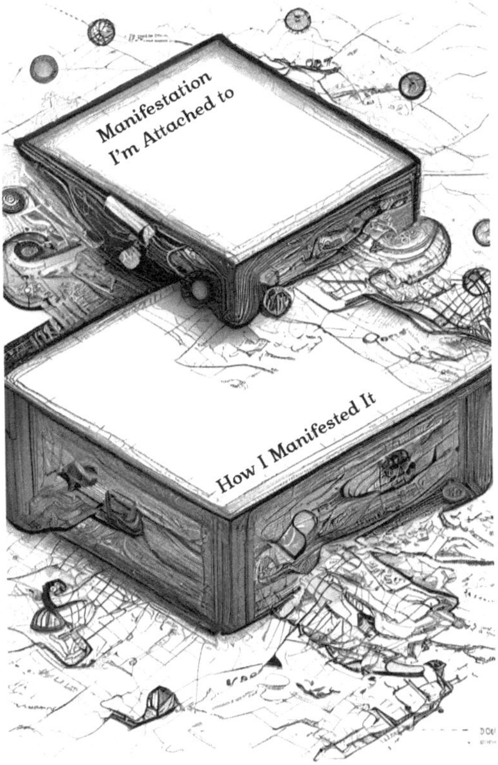
Manifestation
I'm Attached to
How I Manifested It

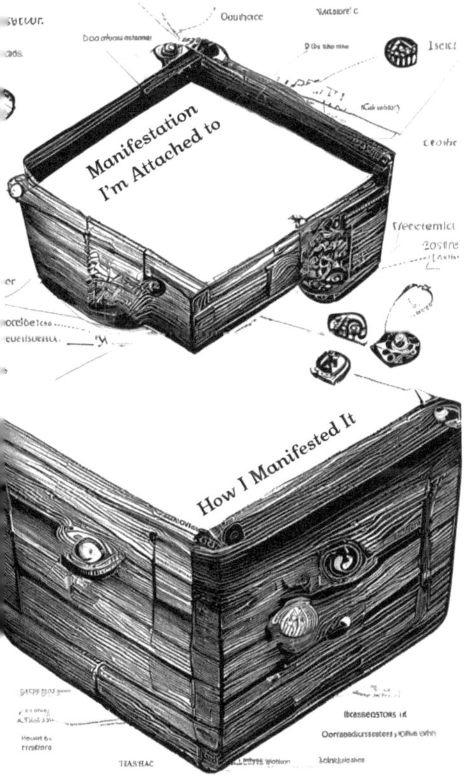
Manifestation
I'm Attached to
How I Manifested It

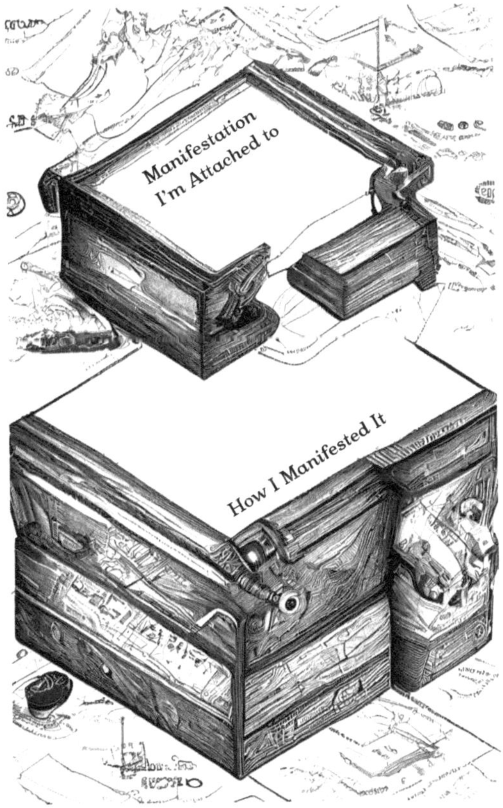
Manifestation
I'm Attached to
How I Manifested It

Manifestation
I'm Attached to
How I Manifested It

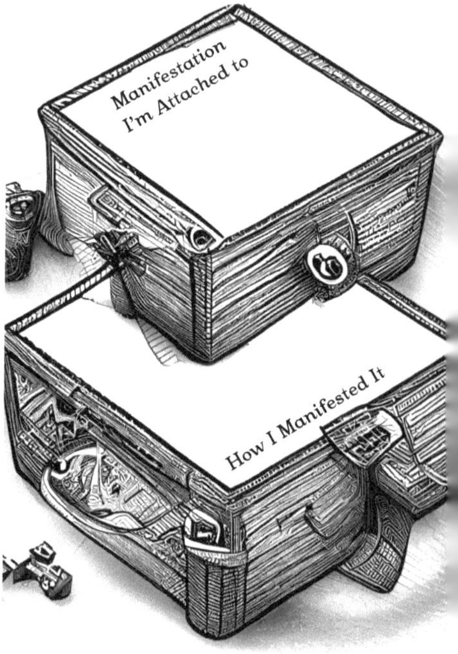
Manifestation
I'm Attached to
How I Manifested It

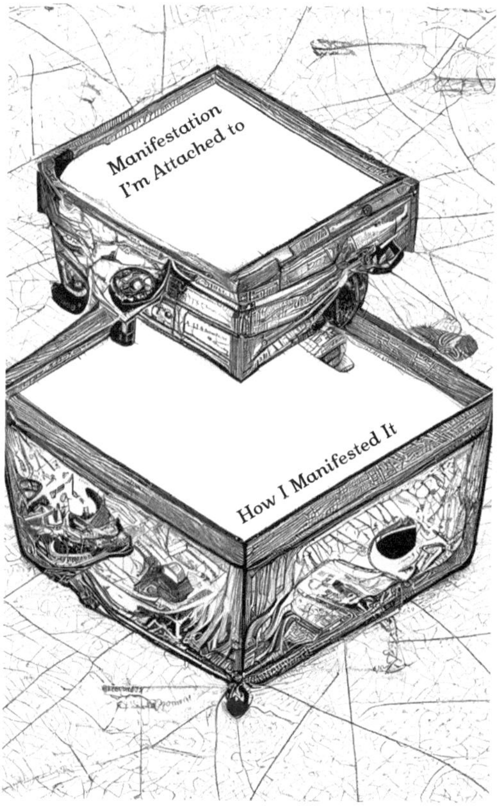
Manifestation
I'm Attached to
How I Manifested It

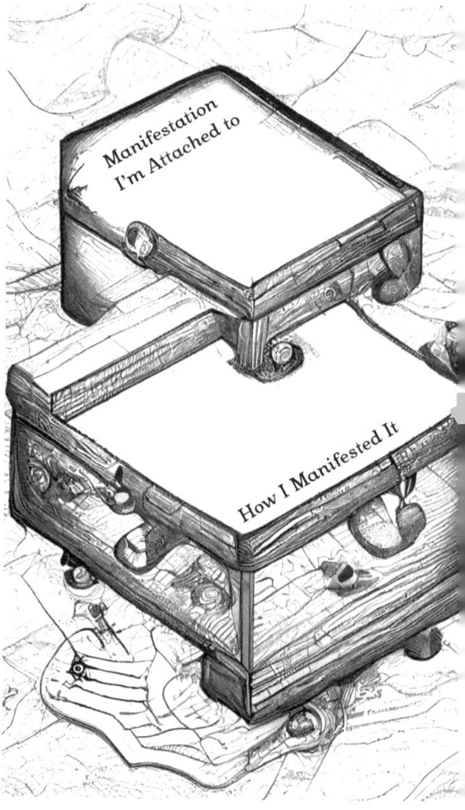
Manifestation
I'm Attached to
How I Manifested It

Manifestation
I'm Attached to
How I Manifested It

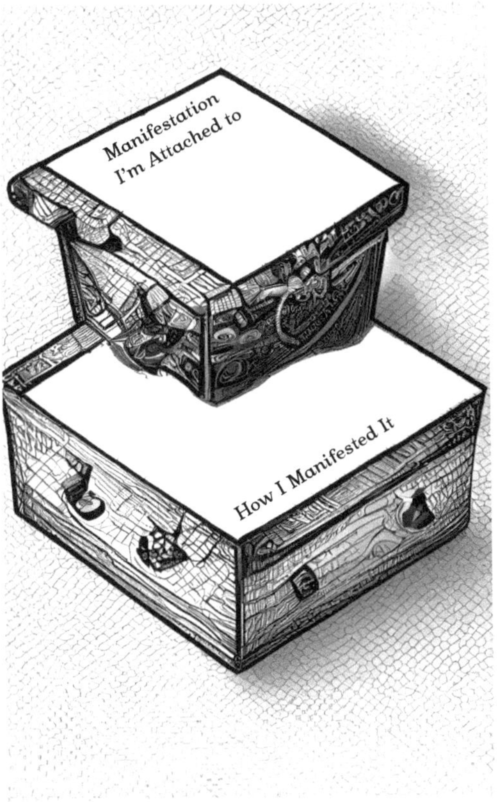
Manifestation
I'm Attached to
How I Manifested It

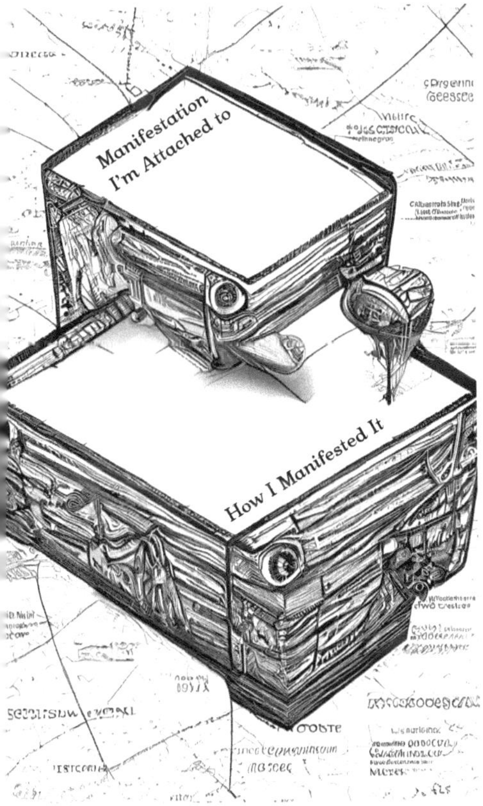
Manifestation
I'm Attached to
How I Manifested It

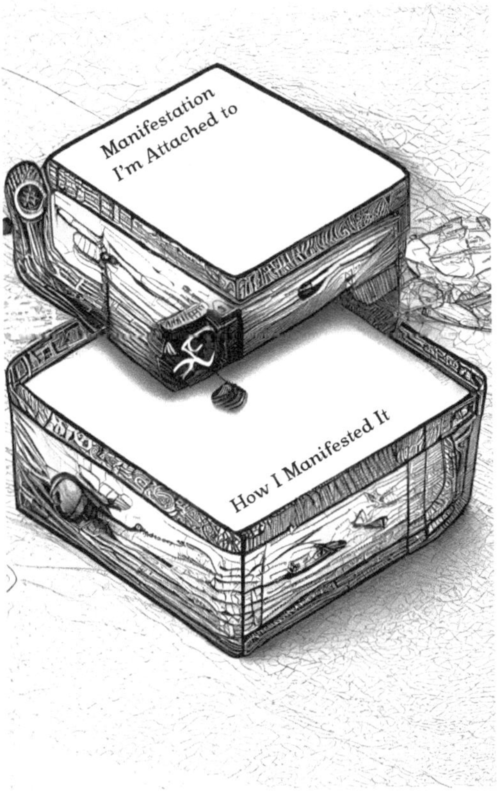
Manifestation
I'm Attached to
How I Manifested It

Notes

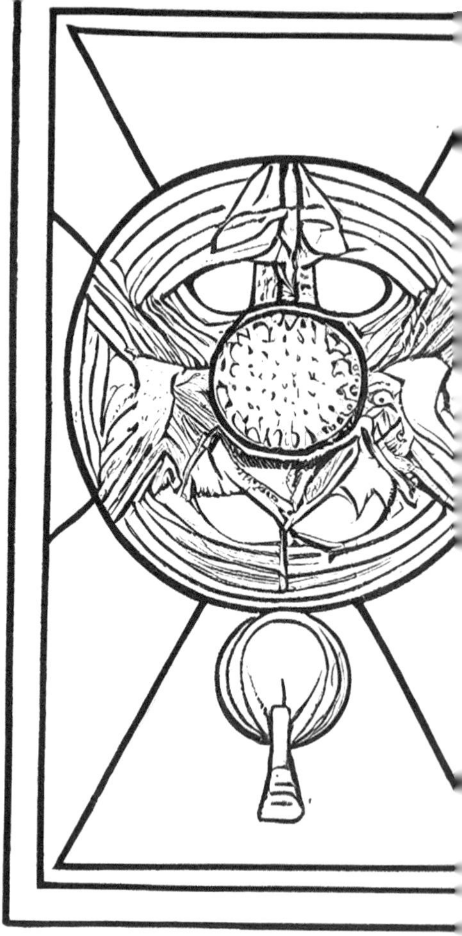

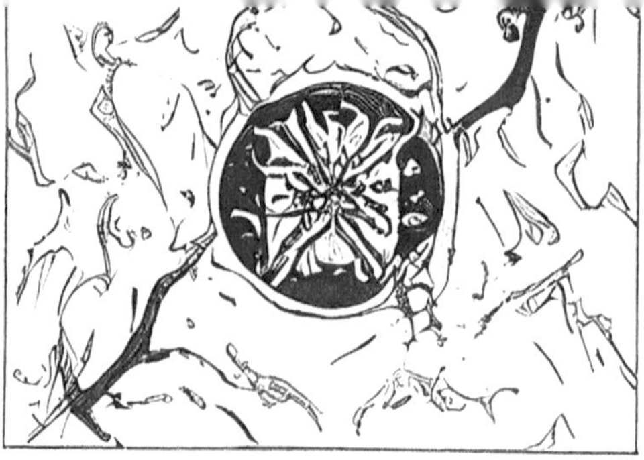

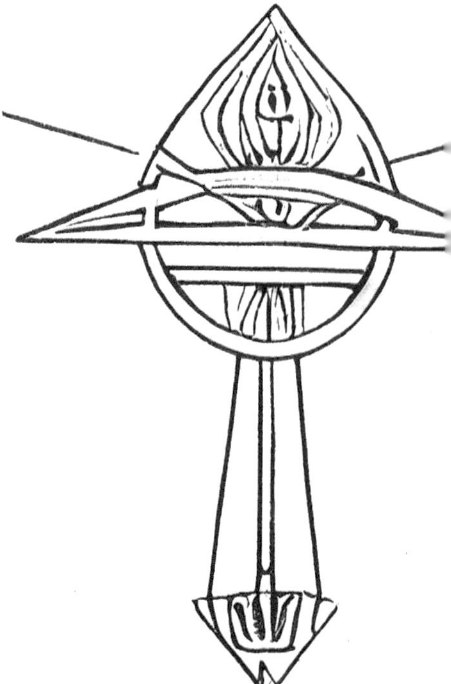

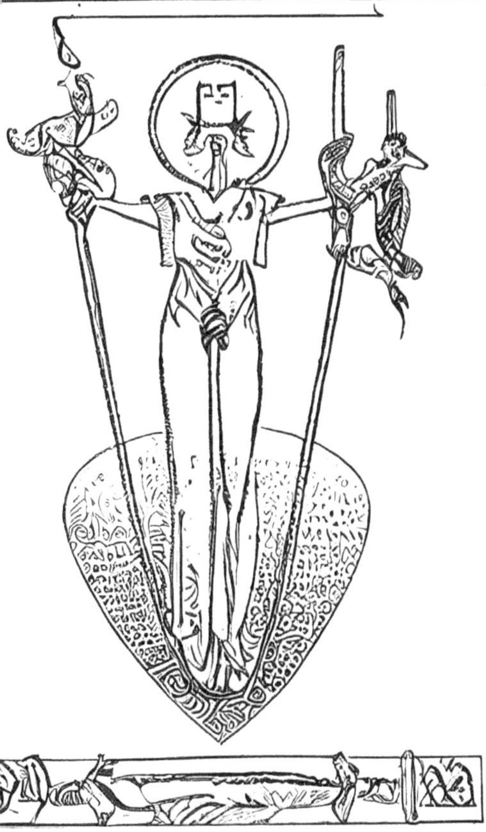

O 'UATIIIIAJ

Woor uetnoqu]

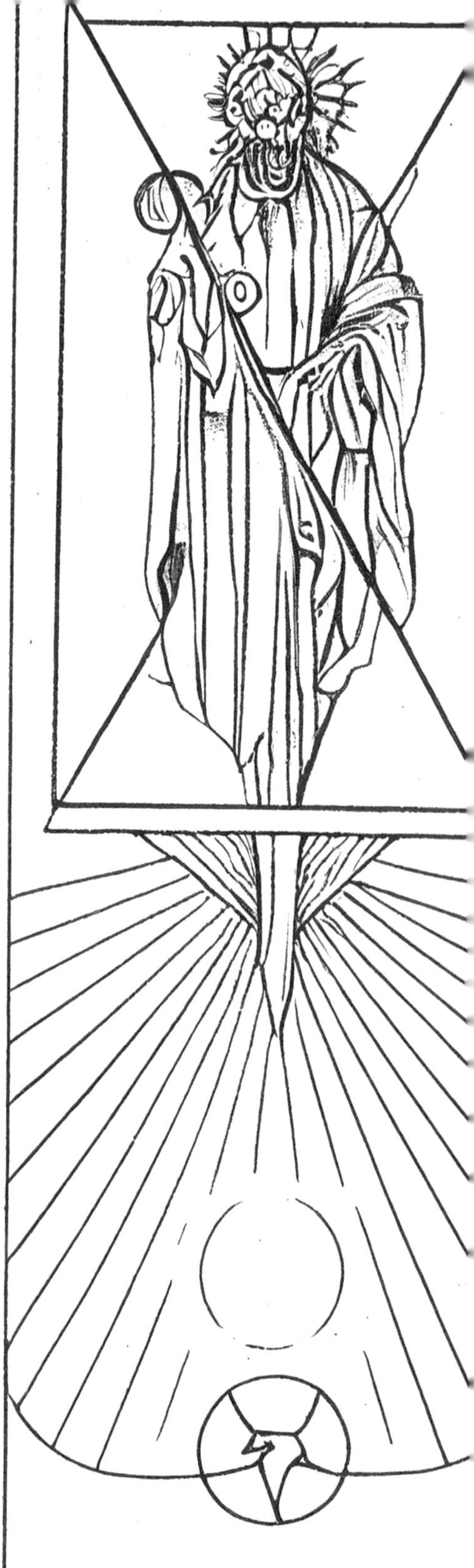

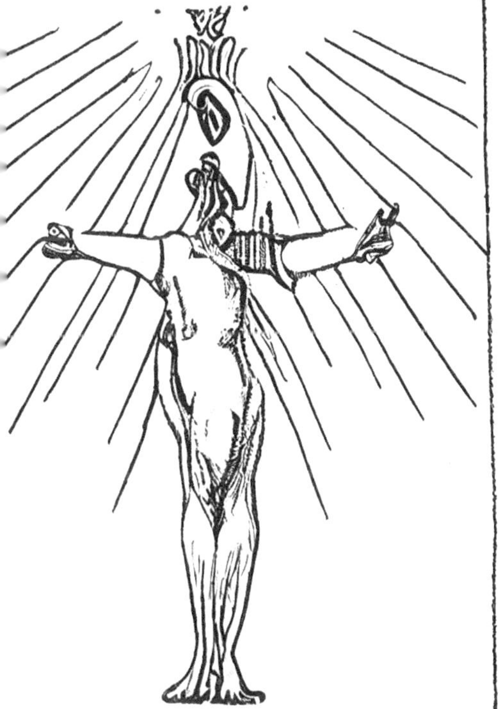

sSLO DS corio cx lntan txtzst croma lnllla
13 Dott ontustaui tr oreol O bo swcoo I o
oi annell LC

I lao tto boaufrlu cnllcrlu rmo lrebcta
abonoeh or bolo ortb o o tusheraala non
oexcol oanlic t on orooui bsl ounr o o
mted Dortvhamcaloooro Ofitco hs2 (vurı